Alternative Food Preservation Techniques

The No Freezing and Canning Guide to Preserving Fish, Meat, Vegetables, and More through Traditional Methods

Table of Contents

Introduction

This culinary journey will take you through time-honored traditions, tapping into the fascinating world of alternative food preservation techniques that extend the shelf life of your favorite foods and elevate them to new heights of flavor and creativity.

Unlocking the Secrets of Traditional Techniques

Explore traditional food preservation methods, where age-old preservation techniques and wisdom meet contemporary kitchens. From the art of fermentation to the tangy allure of pickling and brining, this book's simple instructions and beginner-friendly approach make preserving your culinary treasures accessible.

Elevating Flavors through Smoking Techniques

You'll discover the alchemy of smoking foods to perfection. Whether you are a backyard barbecue enthusiast or a curious cook, this book offers practical tips to infuse your dishes with that irresistible aroma. Learn how to balance the nuances of flavors and transform ordinary ingredients into extraordinary delights.

Nature's Refrigerator for Freshness Year-Round

Unearth the secrets of creating an all-natural cold storage, keeping fruits, vegetables, and more at their peak. The content provided here ensures that even novice root cellar enthusiasts can carry out this age-old but effective food storage practice.

Preservation Techniques for Fruits and Nuts

Explore the techniques of preserving fruits and nuts where summer's sweetness lingers long after the harvest season. With practical tips and methods, this book guides you through making jams, jellies, and nutty concoctions that burst with flavor, tantalizing your taste buds.

Utilizing Preserved Foods

Recognizing the potential of preserved foods, like creating unique condiments to crafting inspired dishes, this book highlights various inventive uses of preserved foods. The engaging content ensures you preserve food and embark on a culinary innovation journey.

This book is your go-to guide, with simple instructions, a beginner-friendly approach, and practical tips. The engaging content transforms seemingly complex techniques into enjoyable culinary experiences. Say goodbye to intimidation and hello to a great culinary experience that tantalizes your taste buds and inspires your inner chef.

Unlike other books that may overwhelm readers with intricate techniques, this book takes pride in its simplicity. The step-by-step instructions are crafted with clarity, ensuring that even those new to food preservation can confidently preserve foods and elevate flavors.

The chapters are structured to gradually introduce you to the world of alternative food preservation, increasing your knowledge and building confidence as you progress. From basic concepts to more advanced techniques, each step is a rewarding learning experience that encourages experimentation in your kitchen. Only time-tested tricks from the experts are included, which significantly impact the outcome of your preserved creations. Gradually, this book can spark your imagination and encourage you to experiment with preserved foods in ways that go beyond the ordinary.

This book is an invitation to a culinary exploration of preserved foods, welcoming everyone who enjoys preserving foods. With simplicity, practicality, and engagement at its core, this book transforms the art of preservation into an accessible, enjoyable, and rewarding experience for every reader.

Chapter 1: Introduction to Traditional Food Preservation

In the hustle and bustle of contemporary kitchens, where speed often triumphs over tradition, lies a culinary art that stands the test of time, known as traditional Food Preservation. Back in the old days, when life moved in sync with the seasons, preserving food was the norm, which provided the required nutrition no matter the weather conditions. As you read through, you'll tap into the timeless techniques that have allowed cultures worldwide to capture the essence of their harvests, preserving sustenance, stories, flavors, and a rich heritage.

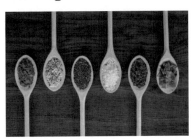

1.   Food preservation requires the use of spices. Source: https://unsplash.com/photos/assorted-color-spoons-with-spices-V5Bqsot6UCg?utm_content=creditShareLink&utm_medium=referr al&utm_source=unsplash

At its core, traditional food preservation is a symphony of salt, smoke, sun, and spices, which can make many foods last longer and deliver their benefits. It's a culinary time capsule, encapsulating the spirit of communities and embodying the vibrant traditions of the past. From the sun-drenched fields of Italy to the snow-kissed villages of Scandinavia, each culture has inscribed its unique chapter in the book of preservation.

While the primary purpose of traditional preservation methods was to extend the life of perishable goods, over time, these techniques were revamped by culinary artisans from the past. Ruby-red hues of sun-dried tomatoes, tangy kimchi, and the savory magic of salt-cured meats are all prime examples of different food preservation techniques, but there are a lot more preservation methods used throughout different regions and cultures. This chapter explores these artisanal processes, each a testament to human ingenuity in turning simple ingredients into culinary masterpieces.

The Evolution of Food Preservation

The history of food preservation techniques is deeply intertwined with the evolution of human civilization. The need to store and preserve food has always been essential throughout history, driven by factors like seasonal fluctuations in food availability, the desire for trade, and the need to ensure sustenance during times of scarcity. Here's a brief background of food preservation through the lens of time.

Ancient Civilizations

During the early civilizations, food preservation emerged as a fundamental necessity. Sun drying, a practice dating back millennia, was employed by societies blessed with moderate climate and ample sunlight to naturally dehydrate fruits, vegetables, and meats. Although sun drying was quite popular in oriental cultures and in the Middle Eastern regions, dating as early as 12,000 BC, the Roman and Egyptian civilizations came to discover the effective preservative powers of salt. They started using salt to preserve their fish, meats, and perishables.

Middle Ages

The Middle Ages witnessed the rise of fermentation as a prevalent preservation technique. Communities across Europe embraced the transformation of cabbage into sauerkraut, the fermentation of milk into yogurt and cheese, and the preservation of various vegetables. Concurrently, pickling gained popularity, with food immersed in vinegar, salt, and spices to ensure preservation, offering sustenance during colder months.

The Renaissance and the Age of Exploration

Advancements during the Renaissance, such as the development of airtight glass containers, laid the groundwork for modern canning. Nicolas Appert's breakthrough in the 18th century showcased the effectiveness of sealing food in airtight jars and heating them for preservation. Smoking, an ancient method, gained renewed significance during the Age of Exploration, proving invaluable for preserving fish during lengthy sea voyages.

The 19th Century

The 19th century marked a pivotal era with the introduction of refrigeration. Ice houses and mechanical refrigeration systems allowed for the storage of perishable foods at low temperatures, extending their shelf life. Louis Pasteur's revolutionary work on pasteurization further enhanced the safety and longevity of liquids, especially dairy products and juices.

The 20th Century

Advancements in the 20th century brought refrigerators and freezers into households, making freezing a widely accessible preservation method. Simultaneously, drying techniques evolved, with freeze-drying gaining popularity for preserving fruits, vegetables, and entire meals.

The Modern Era

In the latter half of the 20th century, the emergence of food additives, including preservatives and antioxidants, became commonplace for extending the shelf life of processed foods. Recently, there has been a resurgence of interest in traditional and sustainable preservation methods. Consumers and producers are revisiting ancient techniques such as fermentation, pickling, and natural drying as alternatives to chemical additives, emphasizing a return to the roots of food preservation practices. Throughout history, food preservation has been an adaptive and innovative process shaped by the needs and ingenuity of diverse cultures. From ancient sun drying to today's cutting-edge technologies, food preservation remains a fundamental aspect of human survival and culinary evolution.

The Importance of Food Preservation

Preventing Food Spoilage

Microbial Control: Preservation methods, such as canning, pickling, and fermentation, effectively control the growth of microorganisms like bacteria, yeast, and molds. By creating an inhospitable environment for these spoilage agents, the freshness and safety of food are preserved.

Enzymatic Inhibition: Enzymes present in food can catalyze chemical reactions, leading to spoilage. Preservation techniques, like freezing and drying, either slow down or halt this enzymatic process, maintaining the quality and integrity of the food.

Oxidation Prevention: Exposure to air can lead to the oxidation of fats and oils, resulting in rancidity and off-flavors. Vacuum packaging and other preservation methods help prevent exposure to oxygen, extending the shelf life of various food products.

Extending Shelf Life

Global Distribution: Preservation enables the storage and transportation of food over long distances. This is critical for global trade, allowing consumers to access a diverse range of products regardless of geographical constraints.

Storage Stability: Techniques like dehydration and canning contribute to the stability of food during storage. This is particularly beneficial for maintaining a consistent food supply, especially in regions where agricultural seasons are limited.

Bulk Purchases: Preservation methods allow for bulk purchases of seasonal produce, reducing the need for frequent shopping trips and ensuring a steady food supply even during periods of scarcity.

Minimizing Food Waste

Extended Usability: By slowing down the natural processes of decay and spoilage, preservation methods reduce the likelihood of consumers discarding food due to freshness concerns.

Economic Savings: Less food waste means economic savings for both consumers and producers. It maximizes the return on investment in agricultural production and reduces the financial burden on households.

Sustainable Practices: Reducing food waste aligns with sustainable practices, as it decreases the environmental impact associated with the production, transportation, and disposal of uneaten food.

Maintaining Nutritional Value

Retaining Vitamins and Minerals: Preservation methods, like freezing and canning, aim to retain the nutritional content of food, ensuring that consumers have access to essential vitamins and minerals year-round.

Diverse Diet: Preservation allows for the availability of a diverse range of foods, contributing to a balanced and nutritious diet. This is particularly crucial in areas where certain fresh produce may be scarce.

Fortification Opportunities: Preservation techniques can be integrated with fortification processes, enhancing the nutritional value of preserved foods by adding essential nutrients.

Enabling Seasonal Availability

Year-Round Access: Preservation methods permit the availability of seasonal foods throughout the year, overcoming the limitations imposed by the natural growing seasons of specific crops.

Market Stability: By ensuring a consistent supply of preserved goods, markets experience greater stability, thus reducing the impact of seasonal fluctuations in the availability of fresh produce.

Culinary Diversity: Preserved seasonal ingredients offer culinary diversity, allowing for the creation of various dishes even when certain fresh items are out of season.

Supporting Economic Stability

Market Flexibility: Preservation provides market flexibility by allowing the storage and release of goods based on demand, mitigating the impact of fluctuations in supply and demand.

Job Creation: The food preservation industry contributes to job creation, from the production and processing of preserved foods to their distribution and sale.

Economic Resilience: Access to preserved foods creates economic resilience, helping communities withstand the challenges posed by unpredictable weather patterns and other factors affecting agriculture.

Facilitating Convenience

Ready-to-Use Ingredients: Preserved foods offer the convenience of readily available, ready-to-use ingredients, reducing preparation time and effort in the kitchen.

Meal Planning: The availability of preserved foods simplifies meal planning, as households can maintain a stock of ingredients with longer shelf lives, minimizing last-minute grocery trips.

Emergency Preparedness: Preserved foods contribute to emergency preparedness by serving as reliable food sources during times of crisis or when fresh options may be limited.

Cultural Preservation

Heritage Continuity: Traditional preservation methods carry cultural significance, allowing communities to pass down culinary traditions from one generation to the next.

Celebration of Diversity: Different cultures have distinct preservation practices, showcasing the diversity of global culinary heritage and fostering an appreciation for cultural differences.

Connection to Roots: Engaging in traditional food preservation methods helps individuals and communities maintain a connection to their cultural roots and culinary history.

The Benefits of Food Preservation

Natural and Sustainable

Traditional food preservation methods, rooted in practices that predate modern industrialization, often utilize natural elements. For instance, sun drying involves harnessing the sun's energy to dehydrate food, while fermentation relies on naturally occurring microorganisms. The sustainability of these methods lies in their minimal reliance on artificial additives and energy-intensive processes. Communities practicing traditional preservation often work in harmony with their local ecosystems, promoting a more sustainable approach to food storage.

Retention of Nutritional Value

Traditional preservation techniques prioritize the retention of nutritional value in preserved foods. Let's take the example of fermentation. During this process, beneficial microorganisms break down complex compounds, enhancing nutrient bioavailability. In the case of sun drying, the dehydration process concentrates nutrients, preserving the original nutritional content of the food. This focus on maintaining nutritional integrity aligns with the health-conscious choices of consumers who seek minimally processed foods.

Cultural Heritage

The significance of traditional preservation extends beyond its practical benefits; it is a custodian of cultural heritage. Passed down through generations, these methods embody the culinary wisdom and cultural identity of communities. The preservation techniques become more than just practical tools; they become a tangible link to the past, connecting individuals with their ancestors' ways of life and creating a sense of cultural continuity.

Reduced Dependence on Modern Technology

Traditional preservation methods are often characterized by their simplicity and reliance on basic equipment. For example, pickling vegetables may involve nothing more than salt, water, and jars. This simplicity reduces dependence on complex modern technologies, making these methods accessible to a wide range of communities, including those with limited access to advanced equipment. This inherent simplicity also contributes to the sustainability of these practices.

Seasonal and Local Adaptability

Traditional preservation aligns seamlessly with the cyclical nature of seasons and the availability of local produce. For instance, communities may engage in large-scale preservation efforts during harvest seasons when fruits and vegetables are abundant. This adaptability ensures a more efficient use of resources, reducing waste and enabling communities to enjoy a diverse and locally sourced diet throughout the year.

Enhanced Flavor Profiles

Traditional preservation methods, such as smoking and fermenting, introduce unique and nuanced flavors to preserved foods. Smoking, for example, imparts a distinctive smokiness, while fermentation creates complex and tangy taste profiles. These nuanced flavors contribute to the culinary diversity of preserved items, creating sensory experiences that are both culturally rich and deeply satisfying.

Cost-Effectiveness

Traditional preservation methods are often cost-effective due to their simplicity and reliance on locally available resources. Minimal equipment is required, and many preservation processes utilize common ingredients like salt, vinegar, or spices. This cost-effectiveness makes these methods accessible to communities with limited financial resources, promoting self-sufficiency and reducing the economic burden associated with more industrialized preservation approaches.

Minimal Environmental Impact

The environmental impact of traditional preservation methods tends to be lower compared to that of industrial processes. These methods typically involve fewer energy-intensive steps and the use of natural elements such as air, sunlight, or microbial cultures. Additionally, the byproducts of traditional preservation, such as pickling brine or vegetable fermentation liquids, are often biodegradable and pose fewer environmental concerns than some industrial waste products.

Preservation of Local Varieties

Traditional preservation practices actively contribute to the preservation of local, heirloom, or indigenous varieties of fruits, vegetables, and other food items. By focusing on preserving regionally-specific produce, these methods play a crucial role in maintaining biodiversity and preventing the loss of unique plant and animal varieties. This preservation of local varieties also supports the resilience of ecosystems and agricultural diversity.

Connection to the Seasons

Traditional preservation practices are intricately woven into the fabric of seasonal cycles. Communities engage in preservation efforts when crops are abundant, aligning with the natural ebb and flow of agricultural production. This connection to the seasons not only ensures the availability of preserved foods throughout the year but also fosters a deeper understanding and appreciation of the seasonal rhythms that shape culinary traditions.

The advantages of traditional food preservation are multi-faceted, encompassing environmental sustainability, cultural richness, nutritional integrity, and accessibility. Each advantage reflects a nuanced interplay of historical practices, community dynamics, and a deep-seated connection to the natural world.

Common Food Preservation Techniques

Although you will be reading about these preservation techniques in extreme detail, here is an overview to get you started.

Dehydration

Process: Dehydration is a method of food preservation that involves removing the moisture content from the food. This inhibits the growth of microorganisms, including bacteria and molds, which are responsible for food spoilage.

Techniques: Dehydration can be achieved through various techniques, including air drying, sun drying, and using specialized dehydrators. Air drying involves exposing food to circulating air, while sun drying utilizes the sun's natural heat. Dehydrators use controlled heat and airflow to remove moisture efficiently.

Applications: Dehydrated foods include fruits (e.g., raisins, dried apricots), vegetables, herbs, and meats (e.g., beef jerky). The absence of moisture inhibits the growth of spoilage microorganisms, allowing these foods to be stored for extended periods without refrigeration.

Fermentation

Process: Fermentation is a natural metabolic process where microorganisms, such as bacteria, yeast, or molds, convert sugars and starches in food into alcohol or organic acids.

Techniques: Common fermentation techniques involve submerging food in brine or allowing natural microorganisms present in the food to initiate fermentation. Controlled environments and specific strains of microorganisms may also be introduced in order to achieve desired flavors and textures.

Applications: Fermented foods include sauerkraut, kimchi, yogurt, pickles, and certain cheeses. The fermentation process not only preserves the food but also enhances its flavor, aroma, and nutritional value.

Pickling

Process: Pickling involves immersing food items in a solution typically consisting of vinegar, salt, and spices. The acidic environment created by the vinegar inhibits the growth of bacteria and microorganisms responsible for spoilage.

Techniques: Pickling can be done through various methods, such as quick pickling (short-term immersion in a vinegar solution) or traditional fermentation pickling. The choice of spices and flavorings contributes to the distinctive taste of pickled foods.

Applications: Common pickled items include cucumbers (pickles), beets, onions, peppers, and various fruits. The acidity of the pickling solution imparts a tangy flavor while preserving the texture and color of the food.

Brining

Process: Brining is a preservation method that involves soaking food in a solution of salt and water. This process not only enhances the flavor but also preserves the food by creating an environment that inhibits the growth of spoilage microorganisms.

Techniques: The concentration of salt in the brine solution, as well as the duration of soaking, can be adjusted based on the specific food being brined. The process is commonly used for meats and certain vegetables.

Applications: Brining is applied to foods such as pickles, olives, and various cuts of meat. It imparts a savory flavor and contributes to the tenderness of meats.

Smoking

Process: Smoking involves exposing food to smoke produced by burning or smoldering wood or other materials. The smoke acts as a preservative, inhibiting the growth of microorganisms and imparts a distinct flavor to the food.

Techniques: Cold smoking involves exposing food to smoke without heat, while hot smoking combines smoke and heat to cook and preserve the food. Different types of wood contribute unique flavors to the smoked food.

Applications: Commonly smoked foods include fish, meats (e.g., smoked ham, bacon), cheese, and certain vegetables. The smoking process enhances the preserved items' taste, aroma, and shelf life.

Root Cellaring

Process: Root cellaring is a traditional method of storing fruits and vegetables in cool, dark, and humid environments, often underground or in insulated spaces. This method utilizes natural conditions to slow down the ripening and decaying processes.

Techniques: Root cellars are designed to maintain a consistent temperature and humidity level. Ventilation and insulation play a crucial role in creating an environment suitable for storing root vegetables, fruits, and other produce.

Applications: Root cellaring is commonly used for storing potatoes, carrots, apples, onions, and other root vegetables. The cool, dark environment helps extend the shelf life of these items, allowing for year-round consumption.

Preservation Techniques for Fruits and Nuts

Canning

This is a preservation method that involves sealing fruits and nuts in jars or cans after heat processing. The heat kills or inactivates spoilage microorganisms, creating a vacuum seal that prevents recontamination.

Techniques: Fruits and nuts are prepared, packed into jars, and then sealed. The sealed jars are then processed in either boiling water or a pressure canner to ensure the destruction of microorganisms.

Applications: Canning is suitable for preserving fruits like peaches, berries, and cherries, as well as certain nuts. The preserved items can be stored at room temperature for extended periods.

Jam and Jelly Making

Making jams and jellies involves cooking fruits with sugar to create a thick, sweet spread. The high sugar content acts as a preservative, preventing the growth of spoilage microorganisms.

Techniques: Fruits are either crushed or chopped, combined with sugar, and cooked to achieve the desired consistency. The hot mixture is then poured into jars and sealed.

Applications: Common examples include strawberry jam, raspberry jelly, and apricot preserves. The sugar content not only preserves the fruit but also enhances its flavor.

Freezing

Freezing is a preservation method that involves lowering the temperature of fruits and nuts in order to inhibit enzyme activity and microbial growth. This process maintains the quality of the items by preventing deterioration.

Techniques: Fruits and nuts are either cleaned, peeled, sliced, or left whole, depending on preference. They are then packaged in airtight containers or sealed bags before being placed in the freezer.

Applications: Freezing is suitable for a wide range of fruits, including berries, mangoes, and certain nuts. The frozen items retain their nutritional value and can be stored for an extended period.

Drying

Drying fruits and nuts involves removing moisture, thus inhibiting microbial growth and extending shelf life. Dried fruits and nuts can either be consumed as snacks or used in cooking and baking.

Techniques: Fruits are sliced or halved, and nuts may be left whole or chopped. They are then dehydrated using methods such as air drying, sun drying, or dehydrators until they reach the desired level of dryness.

Applications: Examples of dried fruits include raisins (dried grapes), dried apricots, and dried apples. Dried nuts, such as almonds and walnuts, are also common snacks and ingredients in various dishes.

Now that you've covered the basics, let's explore the rest of the chapters, learn more about different preservation techniques, understand the process, and then try them to preserve the foods you want.

Chapter 2: Dehydration: The Art of Drying Food

Drying food is one of the most effective food preservation techniques that protect it from spoilage. Back in the day, ancient cultures didn't have refrigerators or the technology to prevent mold and bacteria from spoiling their food, so they relied on dehydration techniques.

2. Vegetables, like mushrooms, can be dehydrated. Source: https://unsplash.com/photos/brown-and-black-coffee-beans-in-brown-wooden-bowl-DCLvx6xP22U?utm_content=creditShareLink&utm_medium=referral&utm_source=unsplash

This chapter explains dehydration as a preservation method, along with its benefits. It also describes the equipment and tools required for effective drying, with step-by-step instructions for drying fish, meat, and vegetables.

Dehydration as a Preservation Method

Dehydration (or drying) is one of the oldest and most popular food preservation methods in the world. It involves removing moisture and water from vegetables, fruits, meat, poultry, or fish to prolong their shelf-life and enhance their flavor. This process also makes the food lighter and smaller. Dehydrated food is perfect for camping, hiking, and backpacking because it weighs less than undried food. You can also use this method if you are traveling in a deserted place with no electricity or living off-grid since it preserves food for long periods.

Ancient cultures dehydrated their food by either wind drying, smoking, sun drying, or air drying. These methods were effective in removing the water from the food. However, they may not be convenient in the modern world, especially if you live in a cold climate.

So, why do people preserve their food? Most types of food can be spoiled if not refrigerated or stored properly. Enzymatic reactions, bacteria, mold, yeast, and other microorganisms can affect the quality of the food, making it inedible. Moisture provides an environment for food organisms to grow. Dehydration reduces the moisture in the food drastically, decreases enzymatic reactions, prevents microorganism growth, and protects it from spoilage.

How Dehydrating Works

Food is dehydrated through steady airflow and low heat, which causes evaporation and releases moisture to prevent the growth of mold, yeast, and bacteria. For this reason, you should leave adequate space between the vegetables, fish, and meat pieces during dehydration in order to allow for the air to easily flow and dry the food. The low temperature also gives the food time to slowly dehydrate without overcooking.

Different Dehydration Methods

There are different dehydration methods: some are outdated, while others are modern and rely on the use of technology. They are all effective, and you can use the right one for you.

Air Drying

Air drying is a simple technique that you can easily use whether you live in the city or off-grid since it doesn't require any equipment. You can either dry the food outdoors in the fresh air or indoors in a well-ventilated room or attic. It is the perfect method for spices, herbal teas, and leafy greens. You simply need low humidity, strong airflow, and no sun exposure.

Sun Drying

Most ancient cultures relied on the sun-drying method because it is simple and effective. This method involves placing the food under direct sunlight. It requires high heat, long days, and sunny climates with low humidity and 86°F temperature. However, this method may not be for you if you are in a hurry because it takes days for food to be dehydrated. For instance, it can take fruits about a week to fully dry.

Sun drying works better with fruits than with vegetables because fruits usually contain high levels of acid and sugar, so they won't spoil under intense heat. On the other hand, vegetables contain less acid and sugar content, so they are prone to mold formation in the heat.

Solar Dehydrating

Solar dehydrating is an environmentally friendly device that is powered by the sun and doesn't require electricity. It is usually placed on top of a greenhouse.

Oven Drying

Oven drying is a lot faster than sun drying. It takes six to 10 hours to dehydrate the food. It doesn't require any other equipment, and you can do it in your home without going outdoors.

However, ovens aren't cost-effective or environmentally friendly since they are energy-consuming. Ovens also produce brittle, dark, and less tasty food than electric dehydrators.

Microwave Drying

3. *Microwaves are a fast and easy method of dehydration. Source: https://unsplash.com/photos/white-microwave-oven-turned-off-WtxE9xb0vQU?utm_content=creditShareLink&utm_medium=refer ral&utm_source=unsplash*

Using a microwave is a fast and easy method, but it only dehydrates leafy vegetables and herbs. It doesn't work with any other type of food. However, the food usually tastes overcooked.

Electric Dehydrators

This is one of the most popular methods in modern times since it is fast, easy, convenient, and efficient. Electric dehydrators usually include a temperature gauge, a fan for ventilation, a heat source, and a timer. They produce the most delicious and highest-quality food of all the other methods. These appliances dehydrate food faster than ovens.

You can dehydrate different types of food at the same time since the appliance has several trays. Unlike the previous methods, electric dehydrators are pricey and require electricity, but they use less energy than ovens. However, there are many brands on the market, so you will find something within your price range. Expensive ones are more efficient and sophisticated; however, they are also an investment since they will last longer than cheaper brands.

Benefits of Dehydrating Food

Protecting food from spoilage isn't the only advantage of this ancient method. It has other benefits that will motivate you to try it right away.

Seasonal Food All Year Long

Dehydration allows seasonal food to be available at your home all year long. You don't have to wait for summer or winter to eat a specific vegetable or fruit; all you have to do is open your fridge. During the winter, you can make delicious vegetable soup by using dehydrated summer vegetables. You will have a great variety of fruits and vegetables all year long.

No Hassle

Imagine that every time you want to cook a recipe, you find all the ingredients in your kitchen. Wouldn't that be great? You don't have to drive to the grocery store every time you need something. Dehydration saves you time and energy by allowing you to store out-of-season fruits and vegetables in your pantry.

You also won't have to leave the house in the frozen winter every time you need to prepare a meal.

More Nutrients

Do you know that dehydrated food contains more nutrients? Freezing, canning, and other food preservation methods lose between 40% and 80% of their nutrients, while dehydration only loses 3% to 5%.

Dehydration retains most of the natural enzymes, minerals, and vitamins in the food. According to a 2005 study in the Journal of the American College of Nutrition, plums, grapes, cranberries, and other dried fruits have more antioxidants than their fresh counterparts.

All the food you find on store shelves is chemically altered and doesn't contain many nutrients, so you and your family will benefit more from dehydrating your vegetables and fruits than buying packaged food.

Out-of-season fruits and vegetables are expensive and don't taste as good as fresh or dehydrated food.

It's Easy

There is a reason why this method has remained popular for years: it is simple and doesn't require much preparation.

All you need to do is cut the food, blanch it, put it on a tray, and dehydrate it.

Food Remains Fresh

If you live in an area with unstable electricity, you probably worry about your food spoiling. Dehydration keeps your food fresh and safe for consumption for long periods. It gives you peace of mind, as you won't worry about your food going bad, especially when you are away on vacation.

Long Shelf Life

Dried food, especially vegetables and fruits, has five to six years of shelf-life, provided it is stored in proper conditions. This is unlike frozen and canned food, which usually lasts for one to two years.

Improves the Flavor

Draining moisture from food intensifies the flavor, leaving you with a very delicious taste.

Portable

Dehydrated food weighs less than regular food, so it is easy to carry, especially if you are going camping or hiking and don't need the extra weight. You can carry it in your backpack without the need for ice packs. Interestingly, when people travel, they prefer to bring unhealthy snacks, like chips or sandwiches, because they are easier to pack and consume. However, dehydrated food isn't messy, and you can take it anywhere.

Since dehydrated food shrinks after you remove the water, you can also store large amounts of food in small spaces.

It Can Never Be Over-Dried

Since you use low temperatures for dehydration, you can never over-dry your food. Whenever the food requires rehydration, you can put it in a dehydrator for a few minutes, and it's good to go.

Cost-Effective

Everything has gotten expensive, even food. Relying on store-bought products for all your needs will break your bank at the end of the month. Food dehydration will save you a lot of money in the long run and prevent you from wasting your resources. For instance, if you have a garden, you can dehydrate the produce you aren't using instead of throwing it away. Say you planted extra peppers, or millions of zucchinis came off your plants. You can dehydrate them and use them whenever you want. You will also save gas money since you won't have to make frequent trips to the store whenever you need fruits or vegetables.

Free of Chemicals and Preservatives

All store-bought products contain chemicals and preservatives to prevent them from spoilage. However, dehydrated food doesn't contain any additives. You will be in control of the whole process, and you can add whatever you want. Knowing what's in the food you feed your family will give you peace of mind.

Healthy Options

When you wake up hungry in the middle of the night and want to get a snack, what do you usually eat? You will probably eat a bag of chips or the last slice of pizza in the fridge, right? This food won't make you full; it will only increase your weight. Dehydrated food will give you a variety of healthy snacks to eat whenever you want.

If you follow a plant-based diet, then dehydration is the perfect method for you. You can use your dried vegetables to prepare delicious vegan meals.

Prepare for Emergencies

This is probably one of the biggest advantages of dehydration. You never know when a disaster will strike or if you will lose your job and will need every penny you have. You can never predict the future, but you can be prepared for it. Dehydrated food is great for emergencies since it doesn't have a shelf life, and you can store as much as you want. It will also give you peace of mind knowing you have access to well-preserved and healthy food during emergencies.

You can also dehydrate multiple meals for your whole family.

Health Benefits

There are many health benefits to dehydrating food that make it the ideal food preservation method.

- Dried food reduces the risk of prostate, bladder, stomach, and pancreatic cancer.
- It improves digestion and prevents colorectal cancer, hemorrhoids, diarrhea, and constipation.
- It boosts energy because it contains more nutrients.
- It reduces the risk of food poisoning because it prevents the growth of harmful microorganisms.

You Can Dry Any Type of Food

There is a huge variety of food you can choose from, like:

- Flowers
- Herbs

- Bread
- Raw crackers
- Seeds
- Nuts
- Granola
- Tomatoes
- Beef jerky
- Lamb
- Chicken
- Salmon
- Sprouted grains like amaranth, quinoa, barley, buckwheat, and rice
- Vegetables like sweet potatoes, green beans, carrots, kale, and zucchini
- Fruits, like lemons, prunes, pears, oranges, apples, and bananas

Tips for Dehydrating Food

Keep these tips in mind before you start dehydrating your food:

- Wash and prepare the ingredients: Wash the vegetables and fruits very well in lukewarm water. Then, slice or peel them into small pieces so they dry easily and evenly. With fruits, remove the skin and the core. With meat, remove the excess fats and slice them into thin pieces. You don't need to cut herbs. Dehydrate them as small bundles or whole leaves.

- For the best results, choose fresh, high-quality, and ripe herbs, fruits, vegetables, and meat. Avoid damaged or overripe food, as they won't properly dehydrate.

- Some vegetables and fruits require pre-treatment to improve their color, flavor, and dehydration. For instance, fruits need to be soaked in lemon juice to prevent discoloration, and you will need to blanch vegetables to avoid loss of nutrients and colors.

- Choose the right dehydration method for you.

- Constantly check the food while dehydrating to see if it is done or not. Feel the food with a fork or your fingers; it should feel leathery and dry without any water. Dehydration time differs depending on the technique you are using, the type of food, and its thickness.

- Leave the dehydrated food to cool down before you store it in airtight containers, and keep it in a cool, dark place to prevent it from absorbing moisture.

Tools and Equipment for Effective Drying

To produce the tastiest and highest-quality food, buy the best equipment available. Although they can be expensive, think of them as investments, as they have high resale value and can last for decades. You should also consider your goals and interests before buying equipment. Are you dehydrating food for emergencies, outdoor activities, or for an off-grid lifestyle? For instance, if you plan to live off-grid, you will need expensive equipment that can fit large amounts of food, but if you are going camping, you can be flexible on the size and price.

Knife

You will need a good and sharp knife to cut the food before dehydration.

Chopper or Slicer

If you can't use a knife, a chopper or a slicer is your best option to easily slice the food before dehydration.

Chopping Board

You will need a stable and clean surface to cut and prepare your food. Simply place meat, vegetables, or fruits on the board and slice, dice, or chop before dehydrating.

You may be wondering why this list includes two of the most common kitchen tools: a knife and a chopping board. These tools are essential for cutting uniform pieces of fruit, vegetables, and meat. Uniformity is significant for effective food drying. If some pieces are larger than others, they will take longer to dehydrate, which can affect the taste and the texture.

Food Containers

Food containers are necessary for marinating the food before the dehydration process in order to protect it and make it easier to slice. High-quality containers will enhance the food's flavor, provided you choose the right material. Your best options are BPA-free plastic, glass, and top-notch stainless steel. Food containers should be sterilized before use in order to provide a clean environment for the food to soak. You will also need airtight containers to store the food after the dehydration process.

Food Dehydrator

This is the appliance that dehydrates the food and removes the moisture. It is responsible for the whole process, so you must choose one that can produce tasty, high-quality food.

- Look for a known brand that is durable, with a strong design.

- It should have adjustable temperature controls and multiple trays.

- It should offer consistent heat distribution to distribute the heat among all pieces of the food and to prevent having undehydrated patches.

- Choose a dehydrator that is powerful enough to remove the water from the food.

Roll Sheets

Fruits, purees, and other types of food contain high levels of moisture, which can seep through the dehydrator trays. A roll sheet prevents dripping, enhances dehydration, and saves you from the hassle of cleaning.

Food Processor

Some types of food require a processor or a blender to prepare the ingredients before dehydration, like soup, and after dehydration, like garlic powder.

Dehydrating Fish

Now that you have learned everything about dehydration and the tools you need, it's time to put all this information into action. You will start with dehydrating fish.

Tools:

- Food dehydrator
- Sharp knife
- Paper towels
- Large bowls
- Storage containers

Ingredients:

- 1 gallon of water
- 1 cup of salt

Instructions:

1. Smell the fish to make sure it isn't spoiled.
2. Rinse thoroughly under cold water.
3. Gently dry the fish with paper towels.
4. Cut it into 1/4-inch strips, and make sure they are the same size to guarantee even drying. Put them in a large container.
5. Prepare a solution of one gallon of water and one cup of salt, and let the fish soak in it.
6. Leave it in the fridge for 12 hours.
7. Then, discard the salt and dry the fish with a paper towel.
8. Store in airtight containers.

If you prefer to dry your fish using a dehydrator, then try this method.

Instructions:

1. Repeat the first four steps from the previous recipe, but instead of putting the strips in a container, place them on the dehydrator's trays.

2. Leave enough space between the strips to allow for airflow.

3. Set the dehydrator to 145°F and leave it for 12 hours.

4. Check on the fish every two hours to make sure it is drying evenly.

5. When it is done, it should feel leathery.

6. Leave it until it cools down, then store it in an airtight container.

If you don't have a dehydrator, you can use an oven.

Instructions:

1. Let the fish soak in a gallon of water and a cup of salt for an hour.

2. Rinse the fish very well.

3. Oil your oven to prevent the fish from sticking.

4. Preheat the oven to 110°F (or the lowest temperature in your oven) and leave its door slightly open.

5. Add herbs and salt to season it if you prefer.

6. Place it on an oiled mesh screen and leave it in the oven for an hour, then turn it and leave it for an hour. Repeat until it is fully dry.

7. Leave it to cool down, then store it in airtight containers.

Safety Tips

- Don't dehydrate frozen fish because the ice can puncture holes in the fish, causing bacteria and mold growth.

- Dry the fish with paper towels before dehydration.

- Clean the dehydrator after you finish to protect it from bacteria.

- Dry your fish at a low temperature to prevent bacteria growth.

Dehydrating Meat and Poultry

Tools

Dehydrator or Oven

Instructions:

1. Remove the bones, tendons, and fat from the chicken or meat, then cut them into small cubes.

2. Preheat the oven or dehydrator to 140°F.

3. Place the meat cubes on the dehydrator trays. Leave space between them to allow for airflow.

4. Put them in the oven or dehydrator and leave them for four to six hours.

5. Check on the meat every hour with a fork.

6. Once they are done, they should either feel brittle, leathery, or dry.

7. Leave them to cool down before placing them in airtight containers.

Dehydrating Vegetables and Fruits

Before you dehydrate fruits and vegetables, you will have to prepare them first.

Instructions:

1. Rinse them thoroughly. However, if you can afford it, it is better to buy organic fruits and vegetables since they haven't been exposed to chemicals or pesticides, and you can just give them a quick scrub.

2. Peel the fruits and vegetables if you want. Remember, the skin will get tough during the dehydration process, which will affect the texture.

3. Slice the produce into small pieces using a knife or a chopper. Make sure they are all the same size so they dry at the same rate. Cut them slightly thicker since they shrink in the dehydration process.

4. Put fruits like apples and bananas in citrus water to prevent them from turning brown. Fill a bowl with water and lemon juice, then leave the sliced fruits to soak for 10 minutes and gently dry them with a paper towel.

5. If you are drying sugar snap peas, sweet potatoes, or any other starchy vegetable, boil them for five minutes, then soak them in ice water right away to shock them. This step helps preserve their bright colors.

Now, your vegetables and fruits are ready for dehydration.

Drying Vegetables in a Food Dehydrator

Instructions:

1. Empty the bag of vegetables or fruits into a mesh strainer.

2. Rinse with lukewarm water for a few minutes.

3. Shake the mesh strainer to remove the excess water.

4. Place the vegetables in your dehydrator tray and spread them out with your hands. Leave adequate space between them to allow for airflow.

5. Put the trays back in the dehydrator.

6. Set the temperature to 125°F and leave the vegetables to dehydrate for eight to 12 hours.

7. Check every hour and test the texture. If they feel hard, they are done.

8. Let them cool down before placing them in airtight containers.

9. Store them in a cool and dark place.

Drying Vegetables in an Oven

Instructions:

1. Preheat your oven to 140°F or to its lowest temperature.

2. If available, use the convection setting, which is similar to a food dehydrator. It circulates the hot air in the oven and accelerates the dehydration time.

3. Blanch the vegetables until they feel tender (leaving the vegetables in boiling water to scald), then rinse in lukewarm water.

4. Bring a large baking sheet and cover it with parchment paper or a cooling rack.

5. Spread the chopped vegetables on the rack.

6. Put the vegetables in the oven and leave them to dry or until they brittle for six hours.

7. Check on the vegetables to see whether they are dried or not.

8. Take them out and leave them to cool down before placing them in airtight containers.

Tips:

- Don't blanch peppers, zucchini, mushrooms, greens, or raw onions.

- Vegetables that require blanching include winter squash, cauliflower, broccoli, and root vegetables.

- Blanch small amounts of vegetables at a time in the microwave.

- Frozen vegetables don't require blanching.

For centuries, people have been using dehydration to dry their food. Even though people can easily get everything they want from the grocery store, many choose to dry their food instead. Dehydration is a simple technique that produces high-quality and healthy food. It is also easy and fast, and it can save you money in the long run. You can use it with all types of food.

You are in control of the whole process, and you can choose what to add to your food and what to omit. This way, you can guarantee that the food you are serving your family is natural and healthy. Dehydration provides you with all types of fruits and vegetables all year long, so you can create delicious and creative meals whenever you want.

Chapter 3: Fermentation: Cultivating Flavors and Health Benefits

Fermentation is a way to make your food last longer and taste amazing. The process is like magic happening right in your kitchen. In this chapter, you'll learn how this old-school fermentation method turns simple ingredients and foods into something special you can enjoy.

4.   Kimchi is a form of fermented food. Source:
https://unsplash.com/photos/cooked-food-on-stainless-steel-bowl-
M_mDgb8guhA?utm_content=creditShareLink&utm_medium=ref
erral&utm_source=unsplash

Whether it's making sauerkraut, kimchi, kombucha, or sourdough, it's all about letting these microorganisms do their thing to create flavors that pop. In the coming sections, you'll learn about the science behind fermentation, the health benefits, the process of fermenting different foods, and a step-by-step breakdown of bringing this kitchen magic to your table. Whether you're new to cooking or a kitchen whiz, fermentation adds a new dimension of taste to make your food stand out.

The Science behind Fermentation

In fermentation, the protagonists are microorganisms, particularly yeast and bacteria. Yeast, a type of fungus, and various bacteria species are catalysts in this biochemical process. They are living entities, microscopic in size, and play a pivotal role in the entire fermentation affair.

Sugar Transformation

The crux of fermentation lies in the metabolism of sugars. These sugars, present in the substrates (food materials undergoing fermentation), serve as the primary energy source for the microorganisms. These microorganisms metabolize sugars through a series of enzymatic reactions, producing energy as adenosine triphosphate (ATP) to fuel their cellular activities.

Gas Production

As a consequence of sugar metabolism, carbon dioxide (CO_2) is generated as a byproduct. This gas manifests visibly as bubbles in the fermentation medium. The effervescence is a direct consequence of the release of CO_2, contributing to the characteristic fizziness observed in fermented foods and beverages.

Preservation Mechanism

During fermentation, the metabolic activities of yeast and bacteria yield various end products, including organic acids (e.g., lactic acid, acetic acid) and/or alcohol. These compounds function as natural preservatives. Their antimicrobial properties create an environment hostile to spoilage microorganisms, thus contributing to the extended shelf life and preservation of the fermented product.

Breaking Down Compounds

Fermentation involves the breakdown of complex organic compounds in the substrate. This process is achieved through the action of enzymes produced by the microorganisms. These enzymes catalyze biochemical reactions that break down intricate molecules into simpler constituents. The transformation of proteins, carbohydrates, and lipids forms a diverse array of flavor compounds, contributing to the unique taste profile of fermented products.

Microbial Diversity

Fermentation involves a diverse community of microorganisms, each contributing uniquely. The microbial diversity within fermented foods reflects the ecological balance established during the fermentation journey. The interactions between various yeast and bacterial strains create a dynamic environment that influences the fermented product's final flavor profile and nutritional composition.

pH Dynamics

Throughout fermentation, there's a dynamic shift in the pH of the substrate. As microorganisms metabolize sugars, they produce organic acids, leading to acidification. This drop in pH is a key factor in creating an environment conducive to the growth of beneficial microorganisms while inhibiting the proliferation of undesirable bacteria. The careful orchestration of pH levels is fundamental to the success of the fermentation process.

Protein Transformation

The breakdown of proteins during fermentation yields bioactive peptides — short chains of amino acids with potential health benefits. These peptides may either exhibit antioxidant, antihypertensive, or antimicrobial properties. The transformation of proteins through fermentation contributes not only to the flavor but also to the functional qualities of the end product.

Reducing Oxidative Stress

Fermentation can enhance the antioxidant content of foods. The metabolic activities of microorganisms generate compounds with antioxidant properties, helping to neutralize free radicals and reduce oxidative stress. This antioxidative potential may contribute to overall cellular health and protection against chronic diseases.

Metabolites beyond Probiotics

In addition to probiotics, fermentation produces a variety of metabolites known as post-biotics. These include organic acids, enzymes, and peptides. Post-biotics may exhibit health-promoting effects, influencing immune function, gut integrity, and overall well-being. The exploration of post-biotics expands our understanding of the multifaceted impacts of fermented foods on human health.

Flavor Development

Amino acids, the building blocks of proteins, are essential for nutrition, and they play a crucial role in flavor development during fermentation. The breakdown of proteins yields amino acids, contributing to the unique taste profile of fermented products. Additionally, the increased availability of specific amino acids enhances the nutritional quality of the final food product.

Fermentation is an intricate biological process orchestrated by yeast and bacteria. It encompasses the metabolism of sugars, the generation of carbon dioxide, the production of acids and alcohol as preservatives, and the transformation of complex compounds into a spectrum of flavors. This orchestrated biochemical symphony not only preserves food but also imbues it with distinct and often desirable sensory characteristics.

Health Benefits of Fermentation

Gut Health Enhancement

Fermentation introduces probiotics, which are live microorganisms known to confer health benefits. These microorganisms, typically bacteria like Lactobacillus and Bifidobacterium strains, reach the gastrointestinal tract through fermented foods. In the gut, they contribute to developing and maintaining a diverse and balanced microbiota, fostering a healthier environment. This microbial balance is associated with improved digestion, enhanced nutrient absorption, and a bolstered immune system.

Nutrient Boost

The fermentation process transforms complex compounds within foods into more straightforward, more bioavailable forms. For instance, the breakdown of phytic acid during fermentation increases the availability of minerals like iron, zinc, and calcium. Similarly, the synthesis of specific B vitamins, such as folate and riboflavin, is enhanced. This heightened bioavailability translates to improved nutrient absorption, potentially addressing nutritional deficiencies.

Regulation of Digestive Processes

Fermented foods contribute enzymes generated during the fermentation process. These enzymes aid in the pre-digestion of components within the food matrix, facilitating the breakdown of proteins, fats, and carbohydrates. This enzymatic action can alleviate digestive strain, making fermented foods particularly beneficial for individuals with compromised digestive function or conditions such as lactose intolerance.

Allergen Reduction

Fermentation has shown promise in reducing allergenicity in certain foods. Proteins responsible for allergic reactions can be broken down or modified during fermentation. While the efficacy may vary, this could potentially render fermented versions of specific foods more tolerable for individuals with food sensitivities or allergies.

Immune System Support

The gut microbiota plays a pivotal role in shaping immune responses. Probiotics derived from fermented foods contribute to this intricate balance, positively influencing immune function. Stimulating immune cells, such as macrophages and lymphocytes, contribute to a heightened defense against infections and a more resilient immune system.

Reduction of Inflammation

Certain bioactive compounds produced during fermentation exhibit anti-inflammatory properties. For instance, short-chain fatty acids (SCFAs) generated by gut bacteria during fermentation have been associated with the mitigation of chronic inflammation. This anti-inflammatory effect extends beyond the gut, potentially impacting systemic inflammation-related conditions like cardiovascular diseases and metabolic disorders.

Mental Health Connection

Emerging research explores the intricate relationship between the gut and the brain, known as the gut-brain axis. Probiotics from fermented foods may influence this axis, impacting neurotransmitter production and signaling. While the understanding is evolving, there's a growing appreciation for the potential role of fermented foods in mental health, with implications for conditions such as anxiety and depression.

Gut-Brain Communication

The intricate relationship between the gut microbiota and the central nervous system is facilitated by a phenomenon known as microbiota-host crosstalk. Fermentation-derived probiotics may play a role in this communication, influencing neurotransmitter production and signaling. The bidirectional dialogue between the gut and the brain suggests potential connections between fermented foods and mental health, paving the way for future exploration.

Metabolic Signaling Molecules

Fermentation produces short-chain fatty acids (SCFAs) as byproducts of microbial metabolism. These SCFAs, including acetate, propionate, and butyrate, act as metabolic signaling molecules. Beyond their anti-inflammatory properties, SCFAs influence energy metabolism, lipid regulation, and gut barrier function, contributing to the broader metabolic benefits associated with fermented foods.

Nourishing Beneficial Microbes

Fermented foods often contain prebiotic compounds — indigestible fibers that selectively nourish beneficial gut bacteria. The synergy between probiotics and prebiotics creates a supportive environment for the growth of beneficial microorganisms. This dynamic interplay between prebiotics and probiotics is essential for maintaining a resilient and balanced gut microbiota.

Antioxidant Elixirs

Certain fermented beverages, such as tea-based kombucha or wine, may contain polyphenols derived from the original ingredients. Polyphenols, known for their antioxidant properties, transform during fermentation, potentially enhancing their bioavailability and antioxidative effects. This interplay introduces fermented beverages as potential elixirs of antioxidants with diverse health benefits.

Biochemical Catalysts for Digestion

The fermentation process introduces a spectrum of enzymes produced by microorganisms. These enzymes, including amylases, proteases, and lipases, act as biochemical catalysts that aid in the breakdown of complex food components. The diverse enzymatic activity enhances the digestibility of fermented foods and contributes to the overall efficiency of the digestive process.

Cardiovascular Health

Certain fermented foods, particularly those rich in bioactive peptides, may exhibit antihypertensive effects. Bioactive peptides derived from fermented proteins can act as angiotensin-converting enzyme (ACE) inhibitors, potentially contributing to blood pressure regulation and supporting cardiovascular health.

The health benefits of fermentation are multifaceted, ranging from the promotion of gut health and enhanced nutrient absorption to immune system support, anti-inflammatory effects, and potential contributions to mental well-being. The interplay between fermented foods and various physiological systems underscores their potential as a holistic approach to health and wellness.

Fish Fermentation

Fermenting fish is a traditional preservation method that results in unique flavors and textures. Here's an essential guide on how to ferment fish, explicitly using the method known as fish sauce fermentation.

Ingredients

- Fresh fish (typically oily fish, like anchovies or mackerel)

- Sea salt (non-iodized sea salt)

- Optional: Aromatics like garlic, ginger, or herbs for added flavor (customizable to personal preference)

Equipment

- Glass or ceramic container with a tight-fitting lid.

- Weights or a plate that fits inside the container to keep the fish submerged.

- Cheesecloth or cloth for covering the container.

- Rubber bands or string to secure the covering.

Procedure

1. Select Fresh Fish

Choose fresh, high-quality fish. Oily fish like anchovies, mackerel, or sardines are commonly used for fish sauce.

2. Clean and Gut

Clean the fish thoroughly, removing scales and entrails. Cut them into smaller pieces for easier handling.

3. Salt Layering

Sprinkle a layer of sea salt at the bottom of the fermentation container. Place a layer of fish on top, then cover the fish with another layer of salt. Repeat this process until all the fish is in the container.

4. Optional Aromatics

If desired, add aromatics like garlic, ginger, or herbs between the layers of fish. These can enhance the flavor of the fermented fish sauce.

5. Press and Weigh Down

Press the fish down firmly to eliminate air pockets. Place weights or a plate on top to keep the fish submerged in its juices.

6. Covering

Cover the container with cheesecloth or a cloth to allow airflow while preventing debris from getting in. Secure the covering with rubber bands or string.

7. Curing

Allow the fish to ferment at room temperature. The duration can vary, but it is typically several weeks to several months, depending on the desired flavor intensity. Check periodically.

8. Straining

Once the fermentation is complete, strain the liquid from the solid remnants. This liquid is your homemade fish sauce.

9. Storage

Transfer the fish sauce into clean, airtight bottles or jars for storage. Refrigerate to slow down further fermentation.

Tips

- Fermentation time can be adjusted based on taste preferences. A longer fermentation period generally results in a more intense flavor.

- Ensure the fish remains submerged during fermentation to prevent spoilage.

- Experiment with different types of fish and aromatics to customize the flavor profile of your fish sauce.

Remember, fermentation involves live microorganisms, and hygiene is crucial. Follow sanitary practices, and if anything looks or smells off during the fermentation process, exercise caution and consider discarding the batch.

Meat Fermentation

Fermenting meat is a traditional method used for preservation and flavor enhancement. One famous example is fermenting sausages. Here's an essential guide on how to ferment meat, specifically for making fermented sausages:

Ingredients

- Fresh meat (usually pork or a mix of pork and beef)
- Curing salt (containing sodium nitrate or nitrite)
- Starter culture (containing beneficial bacteria for fermentation)
- Optional: garlic, pepper, and other spices for flavor

Equipment

- Meat grinder.
- Sausage stuffer.
- Casing (natural casings, like hog casings, work well).
- A fermentation chamber or a controlled environment for temperature regulation.

Procedure

1. Prepare the Meat

Choose fresh, high-quality meat with a balanced fat content. Now, cut the meat into small cubes or strips for grinding.

2. Grind the Meat

Pass the meat through a meat grinder to achieve the desired texture. Consider using different grinding plates for variation.

3. Mix in Ingredients

Add curing salt, the starter culture, and any optional spice to the ground meat. Mix thoroughly to distribute the ingredients evenly.

4. Stuff the Sausages

Load the sausage stuffer with the meat mixture. Stuff the mixture into casings, tying off links as needed. Don't overstuff; it will rupture the sausage skin, making the filling come out into the submerging liquid.

5. Fermentation

Place the sausages in either a fermentation chamber or a controlled environment where the temperature can be maintained between 70°F and 90°F (21°C and 32°C). The fermentation time can vary, but it usually takes 24 to 48 hours. During this time, beneficial bacteria from the starter culture will start fermenting.

6. Curing and Drying

After fermentation, move the sausages to a curing chamber or refrigerator. This allows for further drying and curing. The sausages can either be air-dried or hung in a controlled environment with proper humidity and temperature until they reach the desired firmness.

7. Maturation

Allow the sausages to mature for an extended period (weeks to months) in a cool and controlled environment. The maturation process contributes to the development of flavor and texture.

8. Storage

Once the sausages have reached the desired maturation, store them in a cool, dry place. Depending on personal preference, they can be refrigerated or hung in a cellar.

Tips

- Maintain strict hygiene during the entire process to avoid contamination.

- Use precise measurements for curing salt and the starter culture to ensure safety.

- Monitor temperature and humidity during the fermentation and drying stages.

- Experiment with different spices and flavorings for unique variations.

Fermented meats involve the growth of beneficial bacteria, which contribute to the final product's preservation and distinctive flavor profile. Always follow safety guidelines to ensure the fermentation process is carried out correctly.

Vegetable Fermentation

Fermenting vegetables is a fantastic way to preserve them while adding unique flavors and promoting the growth of beneficial bacteria. Here's a basic guide on how to ferment vegetables, focusing on a simple method known as lacto-fermentation:

Ingredients

- Fresh vegetables (common choices include cabbage, cucumbers, carrots, and bell peppers)
- Non-iodized salt (preferably sea salt or kosher salt)
- Optional: herbs, spices, or garlic for additional flavor

Equipment

- A clean glass or ceramic fermentation vessel (jar or crock).
- Weights or a plate that fits inside the vessel to keep the vegetables submerged.
- Cheesecloth or cloth for covering.
- Rubber bands or string to secure the covering.

Procedure

1. **Prepare the Vegetables**

   Wash the vegetables thoroughly. Remove the outer leaves of the cabbage and save a few for later use.

2. **Cut or Shred**

Cut or shred the vegetables into your desired size and shape. Finely shred the cabbage for sauerkraut or leave larger pieces for pickles.

3. Salt the Vegetables

Measure the vegetables and add salt. The typical ratio is 1 to 3 tablespoons of salt per 5 pounds of vegetables. Massage or toss the vegetables to distribute the salt evenly. You can also add herbs, spices, or garlic for additional flavor. Mix them in with the vegetables.

4. Pack the Fermentation Vessel

Pack the vegetables tightly into the fermentation vessel, pressing down as you go in order to remove air pockets. Leave some space at the top.

5. Use Brine

If the vegetables don't release enough liquid to cover themselves, make a brine by dissolving 1 tablespoon of salt in 1 cup of water. Pour enough brine to cover the vegetables.

6. Weight and Cover

Place weights or a plate on top of the vegetables to submerge them in the brine. Cover with cheesecloth or a cloth, securing it with rubber bands or string.

7. Fermentation

Allow the vegetables to ferment at room temperature. Depending on your taste preferences, the duration can range from a few days to several weeks. Check regularly.

8. Taste and Store

Taste the vegetables to determine when they've reached the desired level of fermentation. Once satisfied, remove the weights, cover them with a lid, and store them in the refrigerator to slow further fermentation.

Tips

- Experiment with different vegetables and flavorings for a variety.

- Ensure the vegetables are fully submerged in the brine to avoid spoilage.

- Cleanliness is crucial; sanitize all equipment to prevent contamination.

- Fermentation time depends on factors like room temperature and personal taste preferences.

Lacto-fermented vegetables are delicious, and they are packed with probiotics and enzymes that can benefit your gut health. Enjoy them as a side dish, a condiment, or a snack.

Safety Precautions During Fermentation

Every method of food preservation requires following a strict process and taking various preventive measures so the desired result can be achieved. Skipping a step in the process or ignoring the safety precautions can turn your efforts of fermenting food into a disaster. To prevent situations like these, here are some safety precautions you must adhere to.

Thorough Cleanliness

Cleanliness is the cornerstone of safe fermentation. Before starting the process, wash and sanitize all utensils, containers, and surfaces thoroughly. Bacteria introduced during preparation can significantly impact the fermentation outcome.

Non-Reactive Containers

Choosing non-reactive materials for fermentation vessels is crucial. Reactive materials, like aluminum or copper, can interact with acids produced during fermentation, affecting the final product's flavor and safety. Glass, ceramic, and stainless steel are preferred choices.

Hygienic Handling Practices

Practicing good hygiene during ingredient handling is essential. Wash hands with soap and warm water to eliminate potential contaminants. Dirty hands can introduce unwanted bacteria that may interfere with the fermentation process.

Controlled Fermentation Environment

Microorganisms thrive in specific environmental conditions. Maintain a controlled environment by regulating temperature and humidity levels. This ensures optimal conditions for the growth of beneficial bacteria, and it inhibits the proliferation of harmful ones.

Precision in Measurements

Precise measurements are critical for fermentation success. Follow recipes meticulously, especially when using ingredients like salt or starter cultures. Exact measurements create an environment conducive to safe and successful fermentation.

Submersion of Ingredients

All ingredients must be fully submerged in the fermenting liquid or brine. This prevents the growth of mold and undesirable microorganisms that thrive in oxygen-rich environments. Submersion also facilitates an anaerobic environment that is ideal for beneficial bacteria.

Gas Release Mechanism

The gas that is released is a natural byproduct of fermentation. To prevent pressure buildup, use vessels with airlocks or lids slightly ajar. This avoids the risk of an explosion and maintains a controlled fermentation environment.

Regular Monitoring

Regularly monitor the fermentation process for any sign of deviation from the expected course. Look for mold, off smells, or unusual discoloration. Timely intervention can prevent the fermentation of harmful microorganisms.

Refrigeration Post-Fermentation

Once the desired level of fermentation is achieved, transfer the product to the refrigerator. Refrigeration reduces microbial activity, preserving the product and maintaining its safety for extended storage.

Common Misconceptions about Fermentation

Fermentation and Sanitation

The misconception that fermentation is inherently unsanitary needs correction. While it involves the growth of microorganisms, the process is controlled and natural. Proper sanitation practices ensure a safe and clean fermentation environment.

Interpreting Bubbles

Understanding the role of bubbles in fermentation is crucial. While bubbles are a normal byproduct, excessive fizz can indicate over-fermentation. Regularly checking and tasting your ferment allows for a nuanced assessment.

Mold Is an Aberration

Mold is not an inherent part of the fermentation process. Although some harmless surface mold may occur, discarding any batch showing signs of mold is generally recommended, as it can lead to health risks.

Odor Perception

The misconception that all fermentations produce strong odors needs clarification. While some ferments have distinctive smells, not all do. Unpleasant smells could indicate spoilage or contamination, requiring further investigation.

Ingredient Suitability

Not all ingredients are suitable for fermentation. Some may either inhibit the process or harbor harmful microorganisms. Following tried-and-true recipes ensures the safety and success of the fermentation.

Alcohol Production

Correcting the notion that fermentation always results in alcohol is essential. The outcome depends on the type of microorganisms involved and specific conditions. For instance, many vegetable and dairy ferments do not yield significant alcohol content.

By adhering to these detailed safety precautions and dispelling common misconceptions, individuals can confidently engage in fermentation, ensuring the safety and quality of their homemade fermented foods.

Fermentation across Cultures

Asian Fermentation Traditions

Asian cultures have a rich tradition of fermentation, yielding an array of unique and flavorful foods. In Korea, kimchi stands out, while China and Japan are known for their soy sauce and miso, respectively. Indonesia introduced tempeh, and Southeast Asia contributed its distinct fish sauce. Beverages, like Sake in Japan and Makgeolli in Korea showcase diversity, reflecting cultural preferences. Asian baking involves rice-based and steamed buns, and dairy products like Lassi in India offer fermented goodness.

European Fermentation Heritage

Europe boasts a heritage of fermented delicacies. Sauerkraut from Germany, pickles found throughout the continent, and various cheeses from France, Italy, and Switzerland highlight the diversity. European beverages include beer and wine, with traditional sourdough bread as a baking staple. Cheeses, like cheddar, brie, and gouda, are integral to European dairy traditions.

Middle Eastern and African Fermentation

The Middle East and Africa contribute unique fermented foods, like pickled vegetables, olives, and preserved lemons. Traditional beverages, like Tepache in North Africa and Tella in Ethiopia, add a distinct flavor profile. Fermentation in these regions is reflected in bread, such as injera, in Ethiopia, and in dairy products, like labneh and leben.

Fermentation in the Americas

In the Americas, fermentation traditions are influenced by indigenous practices and European colonization. Fermented foods include sauerkraut, pickled vegetables, and hot sauces. Traditional beverages, like Chicha in South America and Pulque in Mexico, showcase the diversity. Fermented foods in the Americas include baking with sourdough variations, including traditional cornbread and occasional indigenous fermented dairy products.

Fermented Foods in Different Applications

Fermentation in Beverages

Fermented beverages globally highlight the versatility of this culinary technique. From the enthusiasm of kombucha to the tanginess of kefir, traditional beer brewing, sake, and fruit-based concoctions, fermentation plays a central role in creating a spectrum of beverages enjoyed worldwide.

Fermentation in Baking

5. Bagels require fermentation. Source: https://unsplash.com/photos/brown-doughnut-with-white-cream-BJiAIqSP5ug?utm_content=creditShareLink&utm_medium=referral&utm_source=unsplash

Baking, which is deeply rooted in fermentation, relies on the leavening power of sourdough. Traditional bread varieties, along with bagels and buns, find their distinct flavors and textures through the intricate dance of fermentation. The symbiosis of flour, water, and naturally occurring yeast results in an age-old baking tradition.

Fermentation in Dairy Products

Dairy products, a staple in many diets, showcase the art of fermentation. Various cheeses, including cheddar, gouda, brie, and blue cheese, owe their unique characteristics to fermentation. Yogurt, kefir, and similar products illustrate the transformative power of fermentation in dairy.

Fermentation in the Food Industry

The food industry harnesses the power of fermentation for mass production. From bread and beer to yogurt and sauerkraut, fermentation is a critical player in creating consistent, high-quality products. Enzymes derived from fermentation find applications in various food additives, enhancing flavors and textures.

Whether it's the effervescent kombucha, the artistry of sourdough in baking, or the myriad cheeses and yogurt in dairy, fermentation remains a versatile culinary technique that is embraced globally. Beyond its gastronomic allure, fermentation plays a pivotal role in sustainability. It curtails food waste by preserving surplus produce, promotes local ingredients, and contributes to holistic health through probiotic-rich foods. From reducing energy consumption in traditional fermentation methods to valorizing food waste, this ancient practice embodies a harmonious blend of cultural heritage and environmental responsibility, weaving a narrative of flavor, tradition, and sustainability on a global scale.

Chapter 4: Pickling and Brining: Preserving in Flavorful Liquids

Step into the lively domain of Pickling and Brining, where flavor preservation takes center stage! In this chapter, you'll explore the craft of creating brines and pickling solutions, delving into the secrets of infusing your favorite foods with an explosion of tantalizing tastes. From crisp cucumbers to exotic spices, uncover pickling techniques that metamorphose ordinary ingredients into extraordinary culinary delights. Grasp the time-honored methods of preserving vegetables, fruits, and even proteins, morphing them into tangy, zesty treasures primed to elevate your dishes. But it doesn't end there – unravel the essence of storing and utilizing these pickled wonders to amplify your meals, injecting a burst of flavor that will have your taste buds rejoicing. Get ready to pickle and brine your way to a universe of vibrant and unforgettable flavors.

6. *Pickling can turn ordinary ingredients into extraordinary cultural delights. Source: https://unsplash.com/photos/clear-glass-jars-with-candies-TZw891-oMio?utm_content=creditShareLink&utm_medium=referral&utm_source=unsplash*

Creating Brines and Pickling Solutions

Composition of a Brine

Ingredients

Creating a brine is a meticulous process that starts with understanding the foundational components. The primary ingredients are salt and water. Choose a high-quality salt, such as kosher or sea salt, as it contributes not only to the preservation but also significantly to the flavor profile. The salt acts as a desiccant, extracting moisture from the food and hindering the growth of spoilage-causing bacteria.

Salt Ratio

Precision in the salt-to-water ratio is paramount. The standard recommendation is a range of 5 to 10% salt by weight. However, the specific ratio depends on the type of food being brined. It's a fine line – too much salt results in an excessively salty taste, while too little compromises the brine's preservative function.

Crafting the Perfect Brine

Introduction of Sugar

Sugar introduces a layer of complexity to the brine, offering sweetness that harmonizes with the saltiness. The type and quantity of sugar are variables that allow for personalization. Experiment with different sugars – white or brown sugar, honey, or maple syrup – to achieve the desired flavor nuances.

Herbs and Spices

Herbs and spices are the soul of the brine, providing aromatic depth and complexity. Considerations include garlic cloves, peppercorns, bay leaves, and fresh herbs like dill, thyme, or rosemary. The selection is an opportunity for creativity, allowing you to tailor the brine to match your envisioned flavor profile.

Tailoring Brine for Specific Foods

Vegetable Pickling

For vegetable pickling, a savory brine is the foundation of success. Optimal choices include garlic cloves, mustard seeds, coriander, and dill, creating the classic dill pickle flavor. Adjust the salt content based on the density of the vegetables being pickled.

Fruit Brining

Crafting a sweet brine for fruits demands a distinct approach. Incorporate cinnamon sticks, whole cloves, and perhaps a touch of citrus zest to achieve a delightful flavor spectrum. The sugar levels can be fine-tuned based on the inherent sweetness of the fruits.

The Brining Process

Combining Ingredients

Creating the brine involves a meticulous blending of salt, water, sugar, and the chosen herbs and spices. Stir the concoction thoroughly until the salt and sugar have completely dissolved. Select a non-reactive container that accommodates the quantity of food earmarked for brining.

Submerging the Food

Place the food into the brine, ensuring it is fully submerged. This step is critical, as it allows the brine to infiltrate the food, imparting its distinctive flavors and kick-starting the preservation process.

Duration and Patience

Brining demands a patient approach. The soaking period varies based on factors such as the size and density of the food. This timeframe is critical for the brine to permeate and infuse its character into every fiber. Patience becomes a virtue in ensuring optimal results.

Storing and Using Brined Foods

Storage

Meticulous storage is imperative post-brining. Place the brined food in the refrigerator, utilizing containers that seal tightly. The cold temperature effectively retards bacterial growth, ensuring both the safety and quality of the brined items.

Usage in Culinary Creations

The versatility of brined foods extends to various culinary applications. Pickled vegetables can be stars in salads, sandwiches or as vibrant components of charcuterie boards. Fruits brined in sweet solutions open avenues for enhancing desserts or serving as unique toppings.

By embracing the intricate art of creating brines with a discerning eye for detail, you unlock a culinary realm where each brine becomes a carefully orchestrated symphony of flavors, awaiting your creative touch to elevate every dish.

Crafting Pickling Solutions

Understanding the Science

Crafting pickling solutions is an art that begins with understanding the science behind it. At its core, a pickling solution is a blend of acids, typically vinegar, salt, and sometimes sugar. The acidic environment not only imparts a distinct tang to the food but also acts as a natural preservative, inhibiting the growth of harmful bacteria.

Acidic Element

Vinegar serves as the primary acidic component in pickling solutions. Choose a vinegar with a flavor profile that complements the food being pickled – white vinegar for a neutral tang, apple cider vinegar for a slightly fruity note, or red wine vinegar for added depth. The acidity level is crucial, with a standard range of 5% to 7%.

Tailoring Pickling Solutions for Flavor Complexity

Salt and Sugar Dynamics

Salt is a key player in the pickling process. It not only contributes to the overall flavor but also draws out moisture from the food, enhancing its texture. Experiment with salt types – kosher, sea salt – and strike a balance that aligns with your taste preferences. Sugar, though optional, can round out the flavors and offset excessive acidity.

Herbs and Spices

Elevate your pickling solution by introducing a medley of herbs and spices. The choices are vast – garlic cloves, mustard seeds, coriander, dill, peppercorns, and bay leaves. The combination is an opportunity to impart complexity, creating a nuanced flavor profile tailored to your culinary vision.

Enjoying the Fruits of Your Labor

Creativity in Pickling

The beauty of crafting pickling solutions lies in the room for creativity. Experiment with ratios, herbs, and spices to tailor the solution to your taste preferences. Over time, you'll develop your signature pickling style.

Utilizing Pickled Delights

The fruits of your labor come to life when you integrate pickled items into your culinary creations. Pickled fruits can be enjoyed on their own, as toppings for desserts, or even in cocktails.

Crafting pickling solutions is a meticulous process that combines science, art, and culinary finesse. From understanding the acidic dynamics to experimenting with herbs and spices, each step contributes to the creation of pickled delights that elevate your culinary repertoire.

Pickling Techniques for a Variety of Foods

Fermentation Pickling

Fermentation pickling relies on the action of naturally occurring lactic acid bacteria to transform raw ingredients into pickles. The process begins by submerging vegetables, such as cabbage, for sauerkraut, or mixed vegetables for kimchi, in a brine. Lactic acid, which is bacteria that is either naturally present in the vegetables or introduced through a starter culture, initiates the fermentation process. This transformation results in complex, tangy flavors and probiotic-rich pickles.

Foods: Commonly pickled foods utilizing this technique include cabbage for sauerkraut, cucumbers for traditional fermented pickles, and mixed vegetables for kimchi.

Hot-Pack Method

The hot-pack method involves pre-cooking or blanching raw ingredients before immersing them in the pickling solution. This accelerated pickling process is suitable for fruits and some vegetables. The pre-cooking step ensures efficient preservation and flavor infusion, making it a preferred method for items like pickled fruits or vegetables with softer textures.

Foods: Fruits, like peaches and pears, and vegetables, such as green beans and beets, are often pickled using the hot-pack method.

Cold-Pack Method

The cold-pack method requires placing raw ingredients directly into jars or containers before pouring the pickling solution over them. While preserving the crunchiness of vegetables, this method demands longer processing time to ensure effective preservation and flavor infusion. It's a traditional method known for creating crisp pickles with well-preserved textures.

Foods: Commonly pickled vegetables using the cold-pack method include cucumbers, carrots, and bell peppers.

Quick Pickling

Quick pickling, a time-efficient technique, involves using a basic pickling solution with a shorter soaking time. The simplicity of the process makes it ideal for those seeking a burst of flavor in a shorter time frame. Quick pickles maintain a fresh crunch, making them versatile additions to various dishes.

Foods: Ingredients like red onions, jalapeños, or thinly sliced cucumbers are commonly quick-pickled.

Brine Fermentation

Beyond vegetables, brine fermentation involves immersing proteins or fruits in a saltwater solution. The brine imparts a unique flavor profile to the ingredients, transforming them into savory or sweet-pickled delights. This method is versatile, allowing for experimentation with different ingredients.

Foods: Proteins, like fish (e.g., mackerel or sardines), and fruits, like lemons, can be pickled using the brine fermentation technique.

Refrigerator Pickling

Refrigerator pickling is a convenient method that involves preparing a quick brine and storing the ingredients in the refrigerator. This skips the traditional canning process, maintaining a crisp texture and offering a quick pickling option.

Foods: Vegetables like cucumbers, radishes, and cauliflower are often refrigerator-pickled for immediate use.

Dry Salt Pickling

Dry salt pickling involves rubbing or layering ingredients directly with salt to draw out moisture and create a brine. This method is common in making preserved lemons or salted fish, offering a unique preservation technique without the use of a liquid brine.

Foods: Lemons and certain fish, like anchovies or mackerel, can be preserved using dry salt pickling.

Vinegar Pickling

Vinegar pickling entails immersing ingredients in a solution predominantly made of vinegar. This method provides a sharp and tangy flavor to the pickles, acting as both a preservative and a flavor enhancer.

Foods: Common choices for vinegar pickling include cucumbers, onions, and various vegetables.

Freezer Pickling

Extreme Detail: Freezer pickling eliminates the canning process, allowing prepared pickles to be stored directly in the freezer. This method preserves the texture and flavor of the pickles for a convenient and quick pickling option.

Foods: A variety of vegetables, such as bell peppers, zucchini, and green beans, can be freezer-pickled for future use.

Pressure Canning

Pressure canning involves sealing jars of pickles in a pressure canner. This method is crucial for preserving low-acid foods, ensuring safety by preventing the growth of harmful bacteria. It's a necessary technique for pickling items with lower acidity levels.

Foods: Low-acid vegetables, such as beets or carrots, and certain protein-based pickles benefit from pressure canning for safe, long-term storage.

Dive into the intricacies of each pickling technique and understand the nuances that make them suitable for different foods and preferences. Whether you're drawn to the traditional crunch of cold-packed vegetables or the probiotic richness of fermentation, each method offers a unique journey for your palate.

Pickling Recipes

Classic Vegetable Pickling

Ingredients: Cucumbers, carrots, radishes, bell peppers.

Technique: Begin by slicing or julienning vegetables. Immerse them in a pickling solution comprising of vinegar, water, salt, and sugar. Customize with garlic, dill, or spices of your choice. The cold-pack method ensures that vegetables retain their crisp texture.

Fruit Pickling

Ingredients: Apples, pears, berries, or stone fruits.

Technique: Craft a sweet pickling solution with sugar and vinegar. Add spices like cinnamon, cloves, or citrus zest for depth. Use the hot-pack method for softer fruits, preserving their natural sweetness through a gentle cooking process.

Quick Pickling for On-the-Go

Ingredients: Red onions, jalapeños, thinly sliced cucumbers.

Technique: Ideal for those pressed for time, quick pickling involves a basic pickling solution with a shorter soaking time. It is perfect for adding a zesty kick to salads, tacos, or sandwiches.

Fermentation Pickling

Ingredients: Cabbage for sauerkraut, and mixed vegetables, for kimchi.

Technique: Harness the power of fermentation by submerging vegetables in a brine. Lactic acid bacteria initiate a natural fermentation process, resulting in complex, tangy flavors. This method requires patience, but it yields unique, probiotic-rich pickles.

Spicy Pickled Eggs

Ingredients: Hard-boiled eggs.

Technique: Elevate hard-boiled eggs by pickling them in a brine infused with chili peppers and spices. The longer the eggs soak, the deeper the flavors penetrate, creating a spicy and savory delight.

Bread and Butter Pickles

Ingredients: Cucumbers, onions, bell peppers.

Technique: A sweet and tangy variation, this brine incorporates sugar and mustard seeds. The slices are pickled using the cold-pack method, resulting in a delightful condiment perfect for sandwiches and snacking.

Pickled Fish (Escabeche)

Ingredients: Mackerel or sardines.

Technique: Common in Mediterranean cuisine, pickled fish involves marinating the fish in a spiced vinegar solution with added vegetables. The fish is then either cooked or preserved in oil, creating a flavorful and aromatic dish.

Asian Pickled Ginger (Gari)

Ingredients: Young ginger.

Technique: Often served with sushi, this pickling technique involves soaking thinly-sliced ginger in a brine of rice vinegar, sugar, and salt. The result is a palate-cleansing condiment with a subtle kick.

Mixed Vegetable Giardiniera

Ingredients: Cauliflower, carrots, celery, bell peppers.

Technique: Hailing from Italian cuisine, giardiniera involves pickling a variety of vegetables in a seasoned vinegar solution. Use the hot-pack method for a well-rounded flavor and a versatile condiment.

Beer Pickles

Technique: A creative twist, beer pickles involve crafting a brine infused with the essence of beer, incorporating maltiness and hoppy notes. The cold-pack method ensures the beer essence permeates the cucumbers for a unique flavor profile.

Storage Considerations

Storage Duration: The longevity of pickled foods depends on the pickling method. Refrigerated pickles typically maintain quality for a few weeks to a few months, while canned or fermented pickles can last well over a year.

Container Choice: Non-reactive containers, like glass jars or plastic containers, are preferred for storing pickled foods in order to avoid reactions with the acidic pickling solution.

Refrigeration: Prompt refrigeration after pickling is crucial. Cold storage inhibits bacterial growth, preserving both safety and quality. Ensure that the jars are tightly sealed to prevent air exposure.

Using Pickled Foods in Culinary Creations

Salads: Pickled vegetables, ranging from cucumbers to beets, introduce vibrancy and tang to salads. Whether tossed into green salads or used to create a unique pickled slaw, their presence elevates freshness.

Sandwiches: Transform sandwiches by incorporating pickled items like onions, jalapeños, or cucumbers. These additions offer a burst of flavor and textural contrast.

Charcuterie Boards: Pickled vegetables, combined with cheeses and cured meats, contribute diverse textures and flavors to charcuterie boards. Their tangy notes balance the richness of other components.

Toppings: Pickled fruits make delightful toppings for desserts, yogurt, or cocktails. Their sweet and tangy qualities enhance a range of sweet dishes.

Dressings and Marinades: The pickling liquid serves as a flavorful base for dressings or marinades. Experiment by combining it with olive oil, herbs, and spices to create unique culinary blends.

Creative Culinary Exploration

Experimentation: Encourage creativity by experimenting with various pickled flavors. Combine different pickled items to create unique combinations, or use the pickling liquid in unconventional ways.

Homemade Condiments: Transform pickled vegetables into homemade condiments. Blend them to create relishes, salsas, or chutneys that serve as versatile accompaniments for diverse dishes.

Pickled Proteins: Venture into pickling proteins, such as eggs, fish, or tofu. The pickling process imparts distinctive flavors, adding versatility to these ingredients for use in various culinary applications.

Avoiding Flavor Overwhelm

Balancing Flavors: While pickled foods offer excitement, balance is the key. Use them judiciously to complement rather than dominate the overall taste of a dish.

Pairing Considerations: When incorporating pickled items, consider their flavor profile. Sweet pickles may harmonize well with savory or spicy elements, ensuring a cohesive and enjoyable dining experience.

Shelf Stability of Pickled Items

Inspecting Jars: Before consuming pickled items stored for an extended period, inspect the jars for signs of spoilage. Look for off smells, unusual colors, or compromised seals, ensuring the safety and quality of the pickles.

Safe Practices: Adhere to safe canning and pickling practices for long-term stability. Proper sterilization methods and effective jar sealing are essential for maintaining the quality of pickled items over time.

Storing and utilizing pickled foods is a nuanced journey that extends beyond preservation. From enhancing everyday dishes to creating unique condiments, pickled delights offer a burst of flavor and creativity to your culinary repertoire. As you delve into the versatility of pickled items, remember to strike a balance in flavors and embrace the opportunity to infuse your dishes with the unique character of pickling.

Exploring Pickled Condiments

Extensive Range: The realm of pickled condiments is a vast and varied landscape, expanding the traditional boundaries of pickling well beyond vegetables. Here, we embark on a journey through an extensive range of flavorful accompaniments that add depth and complexity to culinary creations.

Creative Blends: From the zesty kick of pickled mustard seeds to the intricate dance of flavors found in chutneys and relishes, pickled condiments showcase an artful blend of creativity and culinary expertise.

Pickled Mustard Seeds

Detailed Soaking: The meticulous preparation of pickled mustard seeds involves a detailed soaking process. Mustard seeds are submerged in a brine solution that is enriched with vinegar, salt, and an array of carefully selected spices.

Flavor Profile: Dive into the intricacies of the flavor profile as the pickling process transforms mustard seeds into tiny flavor bombs, delivering not only a burst of tanginess but also subtle, inviting heat.

Usage: Uncover the versatile applications of pickled mustard seeds, whether as condiments for sandwiches, flavor enhancers in dressings or as zesty companions to grilled meats and cheeses.

Pickled Relishes

Meticulous Composition: Crafting pickled relishes involves a meticulous composition of chopped vegetables, like onions, bell peppers, and cucumbers, within a carefully crafted brine solution.

Texture and Flavor: Delve into the interplay of textures and flavors as relishes offer a harmonious balance, ranging from the sweet and tangy to the savory, creating a symphony of taste sensations.

Versatility: Explore the versatile nature of relishes, enhancing classic dishes like hot dogs and burgers, finding their way into sandwiches, or serving as delightful side dishes that complement various proteins.

Fruit Chutneys

Artful Combination: The artful creation of fruit chutneys involves combining fruits, vinegar, sugar, and spices. The result is a sweet and tangy condiment that tantalizes the taste buds.

Complexity of Flavors: Delight in the complexity of flavors as the pickling process weaves together the sweetness of fruits, the acidity of vinegar, and the warmth of spices, creating a condiment with a multidimensional taste.

Pairing Possibilities: Explore diverse pairing possibilities for fruit chutneys, discovering how they harmonize with cheeses, how they elevate the experience of grilled meats, or how they become exquisite toppings for desserts.

Infused Vinegar

Creative Infusion: Delve into the creative process of infusing vinegar with herbs, fruits, or spices, resulting in uniquely flavored condiments that elevate culinary creations.

Culinary Versatility: Uncover the culinary versatility of infused vinegar as it contributes depth to dressings, marinades, and various dishes, offering nuanced bursts of acidity that enhance overall flavor profiles.

Presentation: Experiment with different infusion combinations, showcasing the artistry involved in crafting signature vinegar blends that add an extra layer of sophistication to dishes.

Alcoholic Infusions in Pickling

Boozy Pickling

Innovative Integration: Explore the innovative integration of alcoholic spirits into pickling brines, witnessing how this creative fusion elevates pickles with nuanced complexity.

Common Choices: Examine the common choices for alcoholic infusions, from beer and wine to whiskey or spirits, understanding how each imparts distinct characteristics to the pickling process.

Beer-Infused Pickles

Strategic Replacement: Dive into the strategic replacement of a portion of water with beer in the pickling brine. Explore how this replacement provides malty and hoppy notes, enriching the overall flavor profile.

Flavor Enhancement: Understand how beer-infused pickles offer a unique twist, with the choice of beer influencing the final taste, whether it is a stout, a lager, or an ale.

Wine-Soaked Pickles

Purposeful Choices: Delve into the purposeful choices of selecting red or white wine for infusing the pickling brine, adding fruity and tannic undertones that elevate the complexity of the pickles.

Elevated Complexity: Explore the elevated complexity of wine-infused pickles and how they serve as excellent accompaniments to cheese platters and charcuterie boards.

Whiskey- or Spirit-Infused Pickles

Sophisticated Addition: Understand the sophisticated addition of whiskey, bourbon, or other spirits to the pickling brine, imparting robust, smoky, or rich flavors.

Bold Pairings: Explore how spirit-infused pickles complement grilled meats, enhancing the overall dining experience with an extra layer of complexity.

Creative Combinations

Artistic Exploration: Immerse yourself in the artistic exploration of the world of alcoholic infusions in pickling. Understand how experimenting with different spirits, herbs, and fruits allows for the creation of custom brines that reflect culinary creativity.

Culinary Cocktails: Witness the fusion of alcoholic-infused pickles with mixology, where these unique pickles serve as garnishes for cocktails, seamlessly blending the realms of mixology and pickling in unexpected and delightful ways.

Cautions and Considerations

Alcohol Evaporation

Critical Understanding: Develop a critical understanding of how much of the alcohol content may evaporate during the pickling process, leaving behind nuanced flavors without the full alcoholic punch.

Balancing Act: Emphasize the delicate balancing act required in achieving a balanced brine, adjusting the alcohol content to complement rather than overpower the natural flavors of the pickles.

Exploring pickled condiments and alcoholic infusions demands a meticulous journey into the intricacies of flavors, techniques, and creative possibilities, offering an immersive experience for culinary enthusiasts.

Chapter 5: Smoking: Enhancing Flavor and Preservation

Smoking food is one of the most ancient methods of preservation. This tried and tested technique has been passed down thousands of years among multiple cultures. The beauty of using smoke for preservation is that it takes minimal resources, and it is easy once you know the right methods. Smoking works by removing moisture from the food, which helps prevent the growth of bacteria and fungi. Smoke also helps keep parasites away by making the environment inhospitable for them. The pleasant taste and antimicrobial properties of the smoking process make it one of the most enjoyable techniques to keep your food lasting longer.

7. Smoking food can take a long time. Source: David Reber from Kansas City, USA, CC BY-SA 2.0 <https://creativecommons.org/licenses/by-sa/2.0>, via Wikimedia Commons: https://commons.wikimedia.org/wiki/File:The_Food_at_Davids_Kitchen_175.jpg

Although smoking food can take a long time, it is simple and does not require much equipment. All you need is an enclosed grill, wood, and willpower. Hi-tech smokers can even cut down the work you put in. Considering that this preservation method has been around for centuries, or maybe even for millennia, there has been a lot of time to get it perfected. Smoked meat will usually last for a few weeks, but there are accounts of it lasting up to a year in the right conditions. You will immediately be able to tell when smoked meat has gone bad because of the smell, as well as the rot you will see developing.

When you think of smoking food for preservation, it is likely that images of barbeques and meat pop into your mind. However, plants and cheese can also be prepared by using smoke. Smoking is usually paired with other pretreatments, like applying salt. The combination of salt and smoke has antimicrobial properties, helping get rid of the disease-causing microbes in your food. The reduction of water, heat, and chemicals in the smoke beautifully maintains your food for a long time by getting rid of all the microorganisms that cause rot and decay.

Another added benefit of smoking is that it adds a unique and pleasant flavor. The tastes that some preservation methods create take some getting used to, but nothing beats a beautiful smoky flavor, especially on a great cut of meat. You can play around with different types of wood to see what is most palatable. The complex flavor profiles of smoked food allow you to create delicious meals while storing your food for a long time.

Smoking food can go wrong if your preparation is not done correctly. You must consider sanitation and the raw materials you use for the process. The smoking process can be labor intensive because it takes a lot of time and observation. However, once you have mastered the technique of properly smoking food, you will not regret having learned this preservation method. Smoking is not the longest-lasting preservation process. Packaging and storing your smoked food correctly usually allows it to last for about one to two weeks compared to the months or years of other techniques, but this time can be extended when coupled with cool and dry storage. The smoking process takes a lot of energy for minimal preservation results; however, the taste of the food makes up for what the method lacks in storage capabilities.

Different Smoking Methods

There are various methods of smoking to explore. Experimenting with these different techniques can be a fun weekend project. Smoking food is best learned with hands-on practicality because you will find out intimate details that escape you when reading or watching a video about the process. When you get your hands dirty, you will align with the finer details of the curing, smoking, and packaging processes that you could miss when watching a YouTube short. Each method of smoking has its unique considerations and precautions that you must be aware of. Furthermore, the food you are preserving, as well as your available resources, will determine the smoking technique that you use.

Once you understand the basics of each smoking technique, you can either switch between them or use them in combination for the goals you want to achieve with your preservation. The food you smoke and the taste you desire will guide the smoking process. Furthermore, the type of smoker or grill that you utilize will also help you determine which smoking method works best. Once you have your preparation, wood, food, and smoker ready, you can start the preservation process.

There are three main types of smoking: namely, cold smoking, hot smoking, and liquid smoking. Only hot and cold smoking is useful for preservation because liquid smoke is simply a flavoring that you add to the food to give it that lovely smoky taste, but it has no benefits for prolonging the life of your food. Hot smoking is when the meat is cooked and smoked at a higher temperature over a short period. The heat used for hot smoking is still relatively low when compared to other methods of cooking that range between 225°F and

250°F. Cold smoking takes a lot longer, usually from 12 to 24 hours. The temperature is kept lower than 85°F. This low temperature could cause microbial growth. Therefore, whenever food is prepared using cold smoking, especially for meat, the product needs to be either fermented, salted, or cured. Thus, in addition to having a longer cooking time, cold smoking needs more time for preparation.

The advantage of using hot smoking is that the high temperature kills more microbes. Cold smoking takes longer to prepare, but you keep much of the nutritional value of the meat, which could be lost in hot smoking. The downside of cold smoking is the risk of parasites and microbial pathogens developing. Cold smoking is the tastier option, as the meat develops a unique odor and color. Smoking works by drying the meat or vegetables. Natural preservatives in the smoke also play a part in the method's preservation quality.

When you smoke your meat for preservation, you are linked with a long, unbroken ancestral tradition. This preservation method is one of the oldest to have been developed, dating back to the nomadic hunters and gatherers of the Stone Age. In North America and Scandinavia, smoked fish was common, while in Europe, smoked hams were their meat of choice to throw over the smoldering wood.

Cold smoking your meat is a lot gentler, so it is usually used for fish. Since the temperatures do not reach the high levels required to kill many of the parasites and microbes, cold smoking is usually used for meat that can be eaten raw. Safety recommendations require the internal parts of a cut of meat to reach 160°F before it can be consumed. Vegetables, red meat, pork, and cheese are usually done using the hot smoking method.

There are a variety of smokers available on the market. Some are powered by electricity, while others use traditional wood burning. Each of these smokers has different benefits and produces varying tastes. Smoking differs from grilling insofar as the meat is not placed directly on the heat source. Instead, the smoke that comes from a low fire is used to cook and preserve the food. The cardinal rule of getting a great smoke going is to keep it low and slow. If the fire is too high, you risk burning the meat, and if it is too low, you will not get rid of the microbes and parasites effectively. Smoking usually seals in the moisture of the meat with a tougher layer of flesh that the smoke has hardened. However, if you aim to preserve your meat longer, you may opt to allow it to dry more by extending the time that it spends simmering over the fire.

An offset smoker is a slow cooker that is often used in the Southern parts of the United States. Another name for this kind of slow cooker is a horizontal smoker. The design is simple, with the firebox positioned slightly away from the main center of the cooking space. The contraption looks like your standard closed-lid grill, except there is a smaller section sticking to the side of it where your wood or charcoal fire is made. This durable smoker comes in many sizes, and it will last a long time. The thick metal they are typically made from retains heat well for that perfect slow cook from all angles. It can be a bit difficult to get an even cook because the food closer to the firebox will smoke faster than the food further away from it, which means that you have to keep an eye on your meat and rotate it as necessary. The main downside of this smoker is that you will need to watch your meat like a hawk in order to make sure that it is cooked to perfection.

Alternatively, you can opt for a vertical or box smoker. The difference between the offset smoker and the vertical smoker is where your wood is positioned. Instead of being on the side like the offset smoker, in the vertical cooker, the smoke comes from directly underneath the food. Vertical smokers have multiple compartments stacked on top of one another. The bottom compartment holds the wood or charcoal for the smoke. Modern options include gas and electricity, but that takes away the chemical preservation that wood provides. The chamber above the heat source holds water so that the temperature can be regulated. The above levels have racks for the food. A vertical smoker does not dry the meat as much as its horizontal counterpart does, so the preservation properties are slightly reduced. The benefit of this smoker is that it does not take up much space, yet you can cook a lot of food in it at the same time. Vertical smokers usually have a see-through covering on the door, which allows you to monitor the food without letting the smoke escape. The grill looks like a cabinet or a mini fridge, with beautiful white smoke swirling around on the inside. Furthermore, the temperature is easier to regulate, and the heat is more evenly spread.

Another option is the bullet smoker, which is similar to a vertical smoker and functions much the same way, except this variation is more compact and easier to store. Bullet smokers are great options for you to travel with. These smokers are usually the cheapest option, so if you want to immediately get started on a budget, you can explore purchasing this product. Bullet smokers can be disassembled for easy transportation, and they are an amazing entry-level option for someone who is beginning to enter the world of smoking food. A drum smoker is practically the same as a bullet smoker, except it isn't as mobile, but the design is almost identical. However, there are drum smokers that can be deconstructed for easier storage and travel.

On the higher end of the market are pellet smokers and Kamado grills, which are also known as ceramic smokers. The pellet smoker is much like the offset smoker, with the heat source being on the side, but it is more hi-tech. This smoker combines electrical components with a wood fire. All you have to do is set your desired temperature, and the grill will do the magic of maintaining it. Therefore, you will not have to observe the smoke and rotate your food like you would when using an offset smoker. This smoker uses wood pellets made from sawdust. Pellet smokers are bulky, so they are not easy to transport. Furthermore, they are heavy on your pocket, so you need to be willing to invest a lot for this appliance.

The ceramic smoker holds heat well due to the material it is made from. Therefore, if you get it to its desired temperature, it will stay in that region for a long time. Like pellet smokers, they are bulky and expensive. The firebox is located beneath, where your food is placed, and it can be converted into a regular grill if you want to cook your meat directly on the flame. The variety of pellets available on the market allows you to flavor your food by using different combinations of wood.

Every smoker works on the same principle. You need a heat source that is not directly cooking the meat and a cover to contain the smoke. Regular grills that have a lid can be used for smoking. First, soak your wood in water before placing it over hot coals. This will cause the wood to burn, but it will prevent it from bursting into flames. You do not want a raging fire but a constant flow of smoke. Your fire should be positioned away from the food you are cooking, so place it on one side of your grill while putting the food on the other side. If your grill has a thermostat, you will be able to control the temperature as well. You could also use a meat thermometer to measure the internal temperature of the food you cook.

If you do not have the option to construct or buy a beautiful, enclosed smoker, or if you want to embrace a more sustainable choice, you can achieve similar results over an open fire. You can cold smoke or hot smoke your food over an open fire, depending on how you choose to regulate the temperature. First, construct a tripod with some metal poles or wooden logs. Then, you can either tie your food directly to the tripod or you can elevate a grill with some flame-resistant rope, wire, or metal chains. Keep the food elevated high over the fire you build in order to prevent the heat from grilling it directly but allowing the smoke to engulf the food. Low and slow is the name of the game, so monitor the temperature of your fire. Using this kind of smoking method takes a lot of work and effort, but it can be a fun activity to spend time outdoors. Using this smoking method allows you to create a makeshift setup wherever you are.

Smoking Fish, Meat, and Vegetables

The type of food you cook will change the smoking methods that you use. Beef is not the same texture as fish, so it makes sense that your approach will need to change. Vegetables are in a league of their own because they are not even meat. If you are pursuing smoking your food as a preservation method, the key to getting your food to last longer is the preparation. You want your fish to be smoked until it is dry in order for it to have better preservation qualities. Remember that moisture can be the enemy of preservation. Therefore, before you start smoking fish, you should either dry rub the meat with a lot of salt or you can soak the fish in a brine, which is a water and salt mixture. Whether you use brine or the dry option, this salting process will help kill any of the microbes in the meat.

The texture of fish is delicate, so cold smoking works better. The smoke will help cure the fish, and its chemicals will help combat some of the parasites. Salmon is usually the fish option that people go for, but it can contain roundworms, despite many people eating the fish raw. Therefore, the preparation of your fish is important. You can usually spot roundworms in the meat, but they can be tiny enough that you miss them. You must make sure that you thoroughly cook the fish. Although salmon is the typical choice for smoking, you can use white fish as well. Smoked salmon is usually only cooked to a certain level so that it can still be moist, which is why you find it in vacuum-sealed packaging when purchasing it in a store. This variation could probably last for about a week; however, smoking your fish until it is completely dry can significantly extend its shelf life. A dry-smoked fish can last for about three weeks to a month. The brine's crunchy texture and salty flavor make the fish similar to jerky.

Pork can be a parasite-ridden meat, and it is extremely dangerous to consume if it is not cooked well. Hot smoking is a better option for pork so that you can make sure all the tiny living organisms in the meat are well taken care of. Pork usually takes six to 12 hours to cook in a smoker at 225°F. You will know that the meat is smoked when it changes color to dark brown and when it is firm to the touch. To get the smoke to penetrate deep into the meat, it helps when you trim the fat off. You will see what is called a "smoke ring" when you cut into the meat. The outer ring will be darker than the meat in the center. This acidic layer is what prevents bacteria from entering the meat. If you keep your smoked meats out of the heat and the sun, you can extend the preservation period to months. You'll be able to tell that the meat has spoiled if it has a horrible odor.

When smoking meat for preservation, a good tip to remember is that you want to choose cuts that are not fatty, or else you should trim as much of the fat off as possible. Smoked lamb is delicious, but because the meat has a high-fat content, it will not last as long as a leaner choice of meat, like beef. Fat holds moisture, so the drying that the smoking process does is not as effective when there is a lot of fat present. Many people use thick cuts of meat for smoking. This method is brilliant for a tasty barbeque because you can retain some moisture in the meat while still getting that smoky flavor. There is nothing quite like a tender and juicy chunk of meat coming straight out of the smoker. However, if your primary goal is preservation, this is not the best route to pursue. Cutting your meat into thinner sections so that the smoke can go all the way through, along with draining most of the moisture, extends the life of a smoked cut even more.

Smoking fruits and vegetables does not do much for preservation. Typically, nuts, berries, and seeds are smoked to help them last a little longer. Vegetables are made up of mostly water. Smoking as a preservation method works with three principles: first, by drying the food; second, by adding the preservatives embodied in the smoke; and last, by providing heat to kill microbes and parasites. Although smoking veggies can provide a delicious meal, for preservation purposes, it does not prolong their edible life by much. Cold smoking is the best option for vegetables because, like fish, the flesh is delicate. Depending on the vegetables that you are smoking, the cooking time will be different. For example, peppers take about an hour to smoke, while cabbage takes four hours.

Tips for Achieving the Desired Smoky Flavor

Most of the time, smoking meat is not done for preservation but for flavor. The delicious taste of smoked meat is one of the best parts of this preservation technique. Controlling the flavor of your smoke is all about the wood you choose. Any non-toxic wood will work fine, but the smaller details allow you to put on your master chef jacket. Oak is brilliant for beginners because it has a mild and forgiving flavor. The smoke is not overpowering for people just getting used to the taste.

Hickory is a common choice that goes with most meat, including beef, pork, poultry, and fish. Most restaurants that sell smoked meat use hickory wood. The versatile flavor allows you to switch up your meat or vegetables at will. Using too much hickory can cause your meat to be bitter, so if you are completely drying your cuts using smoke, this might not be the best option. When used in the right amount, it has a sweet and savory, almost bacon-like flavor.

Citrus wood goes great with fish and poultry. The mild lemon flavor comes through amazingly. This would pair well if you use citrus marinade or lemon zest in the preparation of your meat. Pork is also a great option for citrus wood. Both orange and lemon wood give a similar flavor. You can pair citrus wood with hickory or oak because its mild flavor combines well with the other smoke.

Pecan wood has a sweet, nutty flavor. The sweetness suits chicken and pork; however, it can be overpowering, so it is best to pair it with other hardwoods. Applewood is also sweet, but it is milder than pecan. For the apple flavor to penetrate the meat, it is important to smoke it for a long time. If you are not into a strong smoky flavor, then maple is your best option because it is lighter and milder than many other woods. On the other side of the spectrum, you have mesquite, which has an intense and pungent taste. Mesquite should be used if you are planning to smoke your meat for a little while. Alder and cherry wood are your fruitier flavors. Alder goes with fish, especially salmon, and cherry wood is great for chicken, turkey, and ham.

The flavor of smoked meat is all about the wood you choose, coupled with how long you smoke the meat. Smoking your meat longer allows the smoke to penetrate deeper into the fiber of the meat, making the flavor more intense. Milder woods can be used for longer smoking times, while stronger woods with more intense flavors can be used if you are smoking your meat for just a little while. Finding the right blend of wood for you may take some experimenting. There is no exact guide to flavor; it all depends on personal preference. Once you have found what works for you or what is a hit among the guests you entertain, then you can go ahead and crown yourself a smoke artist.

Chapter 6: Root Cellaring: Traditional Cold Storage

This chapter will introduce you to the concepts of root cellaring and traditional cold storage. By reading it, you'll learn what root cellaring is and its advantages and disadvantages. The chapter also explores the ideal storage conditions for root cellaring and cold storage, along with tips and options for preserving root vegetables and fruits through this method.

8. Root cellaring is a traditional form of cold storage. Source: Kotivalo, CC BY-SA 3.0 <https://creativecommons.org/licenses/by-sa/3.0>, via Wikimedia Commons: https://commons.wikimedia.org/wiki/File:Root_cellar_entrance_i n_winter.jpg

Introduction to Root Cellaring

Back in the olden days, people relied on cold storage to preserve their food, just as people do on refrigerators in modern times. Ranging from the coldest room in the house to natural cellars dug into hillsides, these storage spaces were used both during the summer and the winter. Cold storage, or root cellaring, is an enclosed space that keeps food fresh by controlling light, humidity, temperature, and air circulation. Even if it's a natural storage dug into the ground, it will be covered with a porous layer that lets a little air in and out. With natural root cellars, people can use the innate insulating, humidifying, and cooling properties of the soil because they require less effort to maintain.

With the rising prices of food and food-preserving costs, root cellars are becoming increasingly popular. Whether you stock your cellar with your own produce or if you mass-bought one from your local farmers market at the end of the season, it's a great solution for long-term food storage. Root cellaring is particularly loved by those who love to consume organic produce year-round without using preservatives and canning.

In milder climates, people usually harvest vegetables and fruit at the peak of their freshness (regardless of when they have to do it during the year) and store them in the root cellar. In colder climates, they usually plant late-maturing varieties, harvest them just before the first hard frost, and have fresh vegetables and fruit all winter and spring.

If you can't dig into the ground, building or converting a sturdy structure will also do. If you live in an area where tornadoes and hurricanes are prevalent, your root cellar can double as a shelter from the elements.

What Can You Store in Root Cellars?

As their name implies, the primary purpose of root cellars is to store root vegetables like turnips, potatoes, beets, parsnips, carrots, and rutabagas. The cellar environment is ideal for keeping these veggies fresh for a long time. However, you can easily use it to store fruit like apples, pears, oranges, and everything else you would keep in the fridge. People also use their root cellars to store rhizomes and bulbs of perennial flowers as the cold keeps them from shriveling, but they won't freeze during the winter. Additionally, a larger cold storage can be used to store beer, wine, homemade beverages, and even canned preserves.

Advantages of Root Cellars

One of the most pervasive arguments in favor of root cellars is the owner's ability to preserve organic, often homegrown fruit and root vegetables. Grocery stores and markets often won't offer out-of-season vegetables, and even if they do, they won't taste the same as the ones you've preserved naturally in your root cellar. With cold storage, you can secure a six-month supply of varied fresh produce and always have nutritious veggies and fruit at hand. Root cellars will also give peace of mind when it comes to potential food shortages in the grocery store, which has been a growing concern in many countries in recent years.

Alternative food preservation methods like canning and freezing are a lot more expensive. With root cellaring, you can use natural sources of insulation, cooling, and the humidity that comes from the produce itself. With a properly built root cellar, you won't have to worry about cooling the place, and you will use the light sparingly, so your electricity bill won't suffer. Beyond being expensive, canning – more precisely, heating up water and sometimes cooking the produce is also time-consuming. However, with root cellaring, all you need to do is lift your veggies, harvest your fruit, and dry and shake them a little to remove the dirt before putting them in storage.

Root Cellar Types and Locations

The type of root cellar you can build depends on your location. Traditional (in-ground) cellars can't be built in every place. For example, you should never dig a root cellar near a septic system or where high water tables are prevalent. There might also be building permissions to consider, depending on where you live and whether building a root cellar in your area is regulated by authorities. The easiest and most recommended option for larger, traditional cellars is to erect or convert a building connected to the main house or other facilities on the property. This can be in the home's basement, under a garden shed, or a new structure attached to your house. The goal is to have a space with easy access and proper control over the inside environment.

If digging into the ground is an option, remember that sandy soil is always the best. The place must have an elevated slope to lead away excess water and condensation. If the cellar's main purpose is to store produce during harsh winters, the storage must be deep enough that the temperature inside can remain above 32 degrees Fahrenheit (especially if temperatures in your area go below 25 degrees).

If you can dig but have highly saturated soil most of the year, you can put metal garbage cans or barrels into the ground to keep the water away from your produce. If nothing else, you can buy a large chest freezer, bury it underground, and use it as a root cellar.

Ideal Storage Conditions for Root Cellaring

As established previously, root cellars are a rather economical solution because the produce can be stored without electricity. Still, to store food for a long period, your storage must meet a few very specific conditions. The main factors you'll need to consider when looking for ideal storage conditions in your root cellar are temperature, humidity, ventilation, and lighting.

Temperature

For most produce, the ideal air temperature in a cellar is 32 to 42 degrees Fahrenheit, but if you can keep a temperature range of 32 to 50 degrees... even better. While a range of 40 to 50 degrees may also work for some produce, it might shorten their storage life. For example, apples and carrots will stay fresh even at these temperatures, but onions won't keep for more than a month. In areas where winter temperatures dip below 25 degrees, deeper, in-hole root cellars are the best for keeping the temperature in the ideal range. The deeper you go, the less the soil will be affected by the extremely cold temperatures ruling on the surface. This way, your fruit and veggies will have adequate protection from freezing. Moreover, cold temperature slows the release of spoilage-inducing ethylene gas and the growth of bacteria, fungi, and other microorganisms.

In indoor cellars, the air circulation is more limited, and a few different temperature strata will be established. The warmest layer will be near the ceiling, followed by a less warm layer, another moderately warm layer, and so on, until you reach the space near the floor where the temperature is the coolest. With frequent checks and implementing strategies to encourage air circulation, you can reduce the difference between these layers. For this, you'll need several thermometers with maximum and minimum readings to determine the variations and ranges in the different areas of your root cellar if you want a more uniform temperature layout. If you have a varied assortment of produce that requires different temperatures, you can take advantage of the layers as they are.

How to Keep Your Root Cellar Cool

To ensure adequate low temperatures in your root cellar, consider the following:

- Tree roots can damage your cellar's structure and cause more air (cold or warm, depending on the season) to get in than needed. Avoid building a root cellar near tree roots, or if you already have one, remove any trees from the vicinity.

- The cellar must be at least 10 feet deep in order to achieve optimal temperature stability.

- Wood doesn't conduct heat, so it's more suitable for shelving and other structures inside the cellar than metal.

- For outdoor cellars, concrete and packed-earth are the only two foolproof ways to regulate the temperature inside the storage.

- Placing Shelves one to three inches away from the walls encourages air circulation, and helps the temperatures remain level in all areas of the storage.

- Hygrometers and thermometers are great additions as they help you survey the environment and take the necessary steps in case the conditions become less than optimal for your product.

- Shortly after you store your veggies and fruit in the fall, the temperature inside will start rising as the produce will breathe. You can easily get the temperature down by letting in some fresh fall or winter air from outside.

Humidity

As a rule of thumb, the humidity level in the cellar must be high enough for the fruit and vegetables to stay fresh. For most produce, the ideal relative humidity is 90% to 95%, which is much higher than the humidity in most homes. In lower humidity levels, root vegetables would start to shrivel up and, over time, become unappetizing. While plenty of humidity comes from evaporation from the produce itself, it is crucial to monitor the humidity levels as they can go down very quickly, especially if you're letting in cold, dry air from the outside or if you have a closed-up, insulated storage. Natural storage spaces with dirt floors and walls work better in retaining natural moisture. Fortunately, using a small digital thermometer with a built-in humidity reading or hygrometer can help you stay on top of your root cellar's humidity. While you can try to figure out the moisture levels without these tools, you won't get nearly as good of results as you would with them.

If you have a natural root cellar, spread packed earth or gravel on its bottom before you start putting in your veggies and fruit. It will keep your feet dry, but it won't let too much moisture evaporate. If you notice the storage facility getting too dry, sprinkle the earth or gravel at the bottom with water.

The water will start evaporating immediately and permeate the air with moisture. Besides sprinkling the floor with water, you can add water by spreading slightly damp burlap sacks over the floor (be careful not to wet it too much... if you can wring water out of it, it's too wet). Another fast humidifying method is placing water-filled pans on the root cellar floor.

The abovementioned measures are typically necessary during fall when you start stacking your storage space. Basement root cellars are particularly in need of added humidity because they can't retain moisture. On the other hand, if you live in an overly-humid climate and have a naturally dug-in cellar, keeping uncovered root vegetables in bins might do the trick because some water evaporates from them, but it gets replaced by the environment just as quickly. By contrast, if you live in a low-humidity area, the best way to preserve moisture in your produce is to layer them with moss, sand, or sawdust, as this reduces the surface area available for evaporation.

Another crucial thing to remember is that warm air absorbs more moisture than cold air, so the evaporation will be faster. Cold and very damp areas are not ideal for root cellaring because they encourage rot. In these conditions, a slight drop in temperature can lead to oversaturation, where you reach a dew point where the excess moisture can't be retained in the air. This is when condensation starts on the ceiling, walls, and produce surfaces. When root vegetables and fruit become wet, they are more likely to spoil, even at optimal temperatures.

Ventilation

Proper ventilation is another crucial factor in your root cellar, as it will help you preclude mold growth and remove ethylene gas from the space. Some fruits and veggies have different humidity needs, but if you can, store them all in one cellar – you just have to find the right way to please them all. By ensuring optimal ventilation (along with humidity and temperature), you can store and enjoy produce much longer. Some fruits and veggies will still keep in not-so-optimal conditions, but they won't last as long.

The main tenets of root cellar ventilation are allowing air to come in and circulating and monitoring it throughout the entire space. By allowing in fresh air, you can keep the area at the desired temperature. Moreover, controlling air intake reduces excessive humidity, preventing condensation, which leads to mold growth and rot.

Air circulates through a root cellar just as it does through any other closed space. When cool air gets in, warm air travels upward, and cool air remains near the ground. If your cold storage is tightly enclosed or large, you'll need to control both the intake and exit of air so you can remove the accumulating gasses. Here, remember that you should always let more air out than you let in, especially during the coldest part of winter; otherwise, freezing air could get in and damage your produce. For optimal ventilation, the intake for the cold air and the outlet for the warm air should be on opposite sides of the space. If your space is smaller or has natural gas for letting air in, you'll likely only need to add a larger outlet for the warm air. When creating the vents, cover them with mesh to pest-proof your cellar.

However, it's still a good idea to monitor the temperature and humidity in your cellar in order to see whether you need to place additional openings to let air in. If you're storing produce in crates or other containers placed on the ground (and not on shelves), make sure to elevate these so air can circulate underneath them as well.

Changing the conditions in a cellar through ventilation is fairly easy. For example, if the temperature decreases rapidly and it's cold outside, you can cover the inlets either temporarily or partially. During the warmer months, you can keep the hot air out by leaving the inlets closed and the outlets open. With large cellars, it might be a good idea to install a device for measuring temperature and humidity. This will also help you find the nuanced differences between the different parts of the cellar, helping you find the sweet spot for the varied assortment you're storing. For example, by identifying the coldest part of the cellar, you can use it to store the most vulnerable produce.

Lighting

To maintain optimal storage conditions, a root cellar must be dark. However, this doesn't mean you can't have any light in it. Installing proper wiring is recommended, as this helps you find and inspect the produce whenever you enter. While letting in natural light from time to time could also be a solution, it might not work as well. For one, it's never a good idea to let direct sunlight in at any time, as even a little bit of it can accelerate the maturing process of fruit and vegetables and lead to rot. Moreover, if you have a larger cellar that is further away from the natural light source, you will find it easier to look at and inspect produce by simply switching on the light rather than trying to discern in a dim light you would get from outside sources.

Preserving Root Vegetables and Fruits in Your Root Cellar

Successful root cellaring requires a little time and effort to ensure your veggies and fruit remain full of nutrients, and you'll have fresh summer root vegetables in December, juicy, late summer/fall apples in February, crunchy carrots in March, and so on. The process has several steps, from planting through harvesting to preparing food for storage.

Smart Planting

It may come as a surprise to many, but food preparation for root cellar/cold storage begins with planting. For this, you need to determine the type of cellar you have and how you will provide the optimal storage conditions for specific types of produce. Remember... not all fruit and root vegetables can be stored together, so if you have a small space in your cold storage, you might want to think about planting varieties that can be stored in similar conditions if you want to enjoy your harvest for months without having to reach for canning or freezer bags, plant only fruit and veggies you can store in your root cellar.

It is also a good idea to opt for late-maturing varieties instead of early-maturing ones because you'll be able to store them for longer. Choose seeds or plants you can harvest as late as possible in their respective seasons.

Preparing Vegetables and Fruit for Root Cellar Storage

To preserve your produce longer, you must find the balance between harvesting as late in the season as possible and picking them at the peak of freshness. This requires regular checkups and inspections of ripe fruit and vegetables in your garden. To find the ideal state of ripeness, look at the color and texture of the fruit or vegetable (and if you aren't sure, you can taste one, too).

Keep up to date with the weather report during the fall so you can pick your produce before the first hard frost. Freezing can damage some of them (especially the fruit), and it will cause them to spoil easily. Even if only a few are frozen a little, as they start rotting, so will the rest.

Rough handling can also cause spoilage as it leads to bruising. Bruised, cut, and otherwise damaged goods will not keep well even in cold storage. Handle your veggies and fruit gently during harvesting, washing, and placing them into adequate containers or cellar shelves. If you see any sign of bruising or rot when picking or sorting them, put these aside and store only the best specimens. If you only find a few slightly damaged ones, cut out the bad parts and use the rest as soon as possible.

Some root vegetables like potatoes and onions need curing before they can be placed into cold storage. Curing entails storing them at warm temperatures for a few days before cold-storing them. To do this, lay them out in a single layer on a tray covered with a breathable fabric. Place another layer of fabric on top to shield them from too much light, and leave them in a moderately warm, well-ventilated place. After about ten days, gather them into dark containers or sacks and put them into your cold storage.

You don't have to worry about washing your produce. If your root veggies have some extra dirt on them, just shake them, and the dirt will fall off; if it doesn't, brush the dirt off gently with your hands. Washing them would require time and effort for drying – never put away wet fruit and vegetables, as this is the easiest way to encourage rot. After shaking the dirt off, cut the foliage to about an inch above the root. The leaves are typically the first ones to rot, so by clipping them back, you can prevent them from spoiling the veggies.

The easiest way to store root vegetables in a cellar is by placing them into buckets or crates, with layers of peat moss, sand, or sawdust between each layer of veggie for proper humidity and air circulation. Still, be careful not to pile too many of them together, as they generate more heat this way. The middle of the pile will never be able to cool down properly and will spoil easily.

Fruit can be placed into baskets, mesh bags, and other containers that enable proper air circulation. Some fruits, like pears and apples, produce ethylene gas, which can cause them and every other produce in your cellar to spoil. To prevent this, wrap them in paper, as this will slow the release of the ethylene gas and increase the storage life of your produce. Veggies like potatoes are particularly sensitive to this gas, and if exposed to it, they begin to sprout. For optimal cellaring, don't store vegetables and fruit together (in the same container or on the same shelf), even if their moisture and temperature requirements are very close to each other.

If possible (if you have space and if they don't need curing), chill the produce in the fridge for a couple of hours before placing it in cold storage. This will kickstart the process of slowing their ripening and help preserve them longer.

Tips for Storing Your Veggies and Fruit

Some root vegetables (like turnips, for example) release a distinctive and quite overpowering odor, so you will want to place them in a well-ventilated area to prevent their smell from permeating the entire space and making your fruit and other vegetables smell like them.

If you're storing several types of fruits and vegetables, look around the storage area to see how to maximize the space, and place everything in areas where they'll be kept in ideal conditions. For example, humid and cold air tends to accumulate lower to the ground, so this area is perfect for produce that prefers these conditions. By contrast, the area near the ceiling is more suitable for produce that keeps best in a dry, warm environment.

Be careful not to leave any chemicals or anything treated with them (like paint-sealed wood shelves) in your root cellar near your produce. Due to the humidity, the chemicals can be released into the air and absorbed by your fruit and veggies. Moreover, using paint-sealed wood doesn't work as well for providing the optimal conditions (isolation, temperature, and humidity levels).

If you're storing your veggies on shelves, space them out and rotate the shelves within the same area regularly. This way, you'll improve air circulation without changing the storage conditions.

Even if you aren't rotating their positions, make sure to inspect your fruit and veggies now and then, looking for signs of spoilage or rot. Remove any produce with the first sign of going bad in order to avoid further contamination and losing even more produce.

Storing Requirements for Different Fruit and Veggies

32 to 40 degrees Fahrenheit, and 80% to 90% relative humidity:

- Apples
- Grapefruit

- Grapes

- Pears

- Oranges

50 degrees Fahrenheit and above, and 80% to 90% relative humidity:

- Sweet potatoes

32 to 50 degrees Fahrenheit, and 60% to 70% relative humidity:

- Garlic

- Onions

32 to 40 degrees Fahrenheit, and 90% to 95% relative humidity:

- Turnips

- Radishes

- Parsnips

- Leeks

- Celeriac

- Celery

- Carrots

- Beets

38 to 40 degrees Fahrenheit, and 80% to 90% relative humidity:

- Potatoes

Chapter 7: Preserving Techniques for Fruits and Nuts

Do you want your fruits to retain their fresh taste even after a week or two? Did you end up with a boatload of nuts that you cannot hope to consume even in a year? The good news is you can preserve them to make them last longer without using any harmful chemicals. Preserving fruits and nuts is slightly different from that of other food products. Fruits tend to decay much quicker, but their freshness can be maintained for long periods.

9.   *Fruits and nuts can be preserved in many ways. Source:*
https://unsplash.com/photos/two-apples-and-walnuts-on-white-
towel-
BCApK6UYl3A?utm_content=creditShareLink&utm_medium=refer
ral&utm_source=unsplash

This chapter will show you many different preservation techniques. You will start by exploring the traditional methods of fruit preservation, followed by the optimum ways to store nuts. And, like the cherry on the cake, you will learn a few creative recipes involving preserved fruits and nuts near the end.

Traditional Methods for Preserving Fruits

It is said that food preservation originated in 12,000 BC, even before agriculture was a thing. The techniques were primitive, and it was generally done with help from naturally occurring elements. Surprisingly, they are as effective today as they were back then.

Drying

Drying is the earliest form of preserving fruits. Back in the day, people used to keep fruits in direct sunlight, exposing them to its warm rays. Combined with the wind and a fire nearby, their moisture was removed in a short time. The idea is to limit the growth of harmful bacteria and enzymes, which mainly thrive on the water content in the fruits. The process doesn't affect their nutritional value by a noticeable margin.

You can use the same technique to dehydrate your fruits, but it may take several days to remove all the moisture, depending on the weather conditions. Alternatively, you can use a dehydrator. The drying times vary, depending on the type of fruit. For instance, apples can be dehydrated within eight hours, but it may take more than a day to dry grapes.

Before placing fruits in the dehydrator, you should peel and slice them. The more the moisture content, the larger the slices should be. If you cut small slices of watermelon, which consists mostly of water, you will only end up with tiny dregs after the drying process.

A pro tip: Boil the fruit in water for a few minutes and transfer it to cold water before placing it in a dehydrator for faster drying.

To get high-quality dry fruits, it is recommended to dip them in vitamin-C-rich liquids like orange juice or ascorbic acid. You can also blanch them in steam or cook them, but you may lose some of their flavor. Once the fruit has been sufficiently dried in the dehydrator, don't directly proceed to store it. Condition it by placing it in a sealed glass container and shaking it for a few minutes every single day for up to 10 days.

Freezing

This ultimate, multipurpose preservation method can also be used for fruits. Many of the most delicious fruits are seasonal, but by freezing them, you can savor their taste at any given time of the year. Did you know that frozen fruits can be preserved for up to nine months? For example, if you want to make apples a part of your regular diet, you don't have to wait until July to get them. If you stock and freeze them in October, you can enjoy them in the spring, too.

A pro tip: Purchase either ugly-looking fruits or perfectly ripe ones for freezing. They are cheap and will retain their ripeness (or become riper) and flavor throughout the freezing tenure.

1. Clean the fruit in cold water and let it dry.

2. Slice it into bite-sized pieces, and remove anything non-edible (skin, stem, etc.).

3. Place only one layer of fruit on a baking sheet and store it in the freezer for about two hours. This step is to ensure that the pieces don't stick together in long-term storage.

4. Transfer them to the plastic container in your freezer or to a heavy-duty plastic bag for long-term storage.

When you are ready to consume your frozen fruit, you can thaw it in the fridge or immerse it in cold water.

Pickling

Pickling makes any drab food delicious, and since fruits are already tasty, their pickles are almost heavenly. Plus, it prolongs the fruit's lifespan to a few months. What makes this method even more appealing is its rich history. From the Mayans of America to the Mesopotamians of Asia, almost every culture used to pickle their fruits in ancient times.

The pickling process has been passed on through generations, and it remains almost the same today as it once was. You need to cut your fruit and drop the pieces into a brine-filled jar. Then, refrigerate it for a few hours before it's ready to be consumed. The brine typically constitutes vinegar and water (50% of each), with salt and sugar added as per your taste.

Almost any fruit can be pickled, but not all may be to your taste. The most preferred fruits are peaches, watermelon rinds, apples, tomatoes, pears, and cantaloupe. Don't pickle under-ripe or overripe fruits. Wait for them to be perfectly ripe so their flavors will mix well with the brine. If the fruit is already decaying and you see the beginnings of mold and rot, there is no point in preserving it through pickling.

Fermentation

This method is also among the oldest forms of fruit preservation. It actually makes the fruit healthier than before, increasing the amount of good bacteria in it. Unlike the other preservation methods, fermentation doesn't retain the fruit's color and flavor, but its nutritional value remains the same. It can be added to alcoholic cocktails for flavor or as a topping for desserts.

1. Start off by making the fermentation syrup in a glass jar. Add water and sugar in a ratio of 2:1, and empty a packet of baking yeast. Mix it well.

2. Shut the lid and leave it as is for around four days.

3. When fermentation begins (bubbles start to form on the surface), wash, skin, and slice your fruit, and then add it to the mixture.

4. Add an equal amount of sugar and stir well.

Sometimes, you may even have to wait ten days for the fermentation to begin. Always look for the bubbles before adding the fruit. Your fermented fruit will be ready at this point, but you can let it lie with the lid closed for a few more days in order for the flavor to develop better. Always use ripe fruit for fermentation. You can use canned fruit, too, but you will need to add it to the fermentation mixture in the very beginning.

Canning

You can easily purchase canned fruits at the supermarket. One big reason is that it helps fruit last longer than other preservation methods. Canned fruit retains its freshness even after a year of canning. Unlike the general perception, fresh fruit isn't simply sliced and directly canned. It is treated with the "boiling-water bath" technique. You will need canning jars and a water-bath canner big enough to hold the jars, along with a couple of inches of water above them.

1. Slice the fruit and immerse the pieces in sugar syrup.

2. Heat the mixture for a few minutes.

3. Transfer it into a canning jar and close the lid.

4. Place the jar in the boiling water bath canner for no more than 20 minutes.

Another, faster method of canning fruit is the "raw pack". You simply have to wash and slice the fruit and place it in a canning jar filled with either hot syrup or water. Seal the jar well. The fruit will float, and its exposed part may darken with time, but it will remain perfectly healthy to eat.

A quick, efficient way to increase the longevity of your fruits is by sealing them in an airtight container. Remember that they will only remain fresh for just a few more days than usual.

Nut Preservation and Storage

Nuts are essentially fruits, so many of the fruit preservation methods are applicable to nuts, too. Unlike regular fruits, however, nuts retain their freshness for several months, but if they aren't preserved and stored properly, they will start decaying long before their shelf life ends.

For Fresh Harvest

If you are harvesting nuts fresh from nature, you can eat them right away, but they won't taste as good as purchased nuts. They may also contain harmful sediments, which may result in food poisoning. To improve their taste and purify them, all you need to do is dry them or freeze them, depending on the type of nut.

- **Almonds:** Freeze for at least 48 hours.

- **Walnuts:** Dry at around 100° for four days.

- **Hazelnuts:** Dry at around 100° for three days.

- **Pistachios:** Freeze for two days before drying at around 150° for 12 hours.

- **Chestnuts:** Freeze to consume within three months. Dry to make them last longer.

For Purchased Nuts

As long as you keep these nuts in their sealed pack after purchasing, they will last for several months. Once opened, transfer them to a new, unused glass jar with a lid. As long as the surroundings aren't too hot or moist, the nuts will remain fresh for nearly six months. If you haven't removed the shells yet, their shelf life will extend to around nine months. Are you using jars that have already been used to store something? You should sterilize them, along with the lid before reusing them in order to destroy any latent germs or bacteria.

What if you don't have any glass jars at all? You can store the nuts in vacuum-sealed bags and place them in the freezer to increase the storage time for up to a year.

Always wash your preserved nuts before eating them. However, if you are drying freshly harvested nuts for the first time, avoid washing them. It will only take them that much longer to dry.

Creative Recipes for Preserved Fruits and Nuts

After preserving and storing fruits and nuts, make sure to finish them before their shelf life ends. Are your jars filled with fruits and nuts that are about to expire, and you cannot hope to consume them all at once? Use them to prepare some amazingly delicious food items. This way, you won't have a problem finishing them in a single sitting.

Jam from Fruits

This is probably the most common method of using preserved fruits. It is more of a preservation method itself since it extends the shelf life by about six months to one year if frozen and up to one month if refrigerated. Apricots and peaches are popularly used for making jam, but oranges, pears, and berries taste good, too. It retains almost all the benefits of the respective fruits and takes no more than 45 minutes to be ready for consumption.

Ingredients:

- 2-3 pounds of fruit
- 3-4 cups of sugar (depending on the sweetness of the fruit)
- 2-3 tablespoons of freshly squeezed lemon juice
- Salt (optional)

Instructions:

1. Add fruit and sugar to a pot (along with salt, if needed) and mix them well.

2. Boil it to dissolve any remaining sugar chunks.

3. Mash the fruit as it boils.

4. Keep boiling and stirring as you pour lemon juice into the mixture.

5. After 10 minutes, fruit chunks will begin to float on top as the surface is filled with foam; turn off the burner and remove the foam layer with a spoon.

6. Pour the mixture into a container and wait for it to cool.

7. Cover it with the lid and store it in the fridge or freezer.

Butter from Nuts

This is another basic recipe that is also a preservation technique but with nuts. Nut butter is a healthy alternative to dairy cream butter. You can prepare it with any of your favorite nuts, but walnuts and almonds are most commonly used. It lasts for close to six months if stored in the fridge, but it is recommended to consume it within three months to experience its fresh taste. This sumptuous recipe below doesn't take more than 30 minutes to prepare.

Ingredients:

- 10-15 ounces of nuts
- Salt
- Honey (as required)
- Pumpkin pie spice (as required)
- Chocolate chips (as required)

- Flavored or coconut oil (if required)

Instructions:

1. Spread the nuts on a baking sheet.

2. Pour as much honey as required and add a bit of pumpkin pie spice.

3. Sprinkle chocolate chips and a pinch of salt.

4. Place the sheet in a toaster oven for around five minutes.

5. Transfer the nuts, along with the seasonings to a food processor; process for around 10 minutes.

6. If the churned butter doesn't look smooth, pour a bit of oil and process for a few more minutes.

7. Store the finished butter in a clean container with a lid.

If nut butter is part of your daily diet, don't store it in the fridge. It will last for nearly a month in an airtight container at room temperature. The best part is, it won't harden but will remain fresh and creamy throughout.

Cakes from Dried Fruits

Making a cake from a bunch of dried fruits is among the most delectable options for finishing your preserved fruits. You can savor the slices with your morning coffee or after an appetizing dinner. With the recipe below, you can bake around six slices with any type of dried fruit, all within 45 minutes.

Ingredients:

- 1 cup of self-rising flour

- 1 cup of desiccated coconut

- 1 cup of milk

- 1 cup of dried fruit

- 1 cup of sugar

Instructions:

1. Mix the above ingredients with a spoon or a blender in a container.

2. Spread the concoction on a baking sheet.

3. Bake at around 350° for half an hour.

To finish your nut reserves, you can insert the pieces into the baked slices.

Smoothie from Frozen Fruits

With frozen fruits, the first thing that comes to mind is a rich, creamy smoothie. It is not only healthy but infinitely tasty, too. You have already done the part that takes the longest time for smoothie preparation: freezing the fruit. After this, it will only take you five minutes to prepare your favorite drink.

Ingredients:

- 2-3 cups of frozen fruits (of any type, depending on your preference)

- 1 cup of milk

- Half a cup of yogurt

- Half a cup of orange juice

- Honey or sugar (as required)

Instructions:

1. Add all ingredients in a blender; add the frozen fruits last to retain their flavor.

2. Keep blending until the texture becomes smooth.

3. You can add more milk or fruit, depending on your preferred texture, and blend again.

It is recommended to drink it right away. However, if you wish to store it for later, you will need to pour it into an airtight container and place it in the fridge. It will stay fresh for no more than a day.

Pickled Watermelon Rinds

When it comes to pickled fruits, few other fruits taste as good as watermelon rinds. They are also the easiest and fastest to prepare, taking no more than a little over 80 minutes. The tangy taste of this summer season's fruit exterior can be enjoyed for a month after the pickle is ready.

Ingredients:

- 1-2 cups of peeled watermelon rinds
- Pickling brine
- Clove and coriander seeds
- Peppercorns

Instructions:

1. Slice the rind into small pieces.

2. Place them in a container and pour the brine over them.

3. Boil the concoction for five minutes.

4. Transfer it into a glass jar and let it cool (it won't take more than an hour).

You can either consume it right away or store it in the refrigerator for more than a month. Did you know that you can pickle the leftover watermelon, too? Use the same boiling, cooling, and refrigerating technique to add a tangy twist to its sweet taste.

Fermented Peaches Pizza

Pizza topped with fresh peaches is nothing new. However, switch to fermented peaches, and the taste will change drastically as its complex flavors get absorbed in the dough. Since you have already fermented the fruit, the prep time will be the same as that for any other pizza (around 20 minutes), provided the remaining toppings are ready, too.

Ingredients:

- Fermented peaches (made from 2-3 peaches)
- Pizza dough (or base)
- 1 (or more as required) teaspoon of olive oil
- Shredded cheese (as required)
- 3-4 pieces of bacon
- A few drops of balsamic glaze
- Any other toppings as needed

Instructions:

1. Roll out the pizza dough to your desired thickness.
2. Place it (or the base) on a baking sheet.
3. Spread olive oil on the dough evenly throughout.

4. Sprinkle shredded cheese.

5. Place slices of fermented peaches, followed by the bacon.

6. Add any other topping as needed.

7. Preheat the oven to around 500° and put the baking sheet in.

8. Let it bake for around 15 minutes.

9. Remove the baked pizza, top it with a few drops of balsamic glaze, and serve hot.

Ambrosia Salad with Canned Fruits

Ambrosia is among the most delicious fruit salads in the country. What makes it special is the inclusion of pineapples and oranges, two fruits available in different seasons. Hence, it is often made from their canned variants. If all the ingredients are prepared beforehand, it won't take you more than 10 minutes to make this delicacy.

Ingredients:

- 20 ounces of pineapple pieces
- 15 ounces of mandarin oranges
- 2 cups of marshmallows
- 1 cup of coconut (shredded and sweetened)
- 1-2 cups of whipped cream
- 1 cup of Greek yogurt

Instructions:

1. Drain the fruits as much as you can with a paper towel.

2. Mix them with the marshmallows and the shredded coconut in a bowl.

3. Take another bowl and mix the whipped cream with Greek yogurt; this will be the dressing.

4. Pour the dressing over the fruit mixture and stir the entire combination until everything is evenly coated with the former.

5. Stretch a film of plastic wrapping paper over the bowl and refrigerate it for two hours. Serve fresh.

You can add your preserved nuts to the mixture either during the mixing phase or after refrigeration.

Almond Biscotti

Give a nutty twist to your breakfast cookies. An almond biscotti is an Italian biscuit that tastes best when dipped in wine. All alone, it has excellent nutritional value, thanks to all the almonds. A healthy batch of three dozen cookies can be ready for consumption within two hours.

Ingredients:

- 2 cups of all-purpose flour
- 1 cup of sugar
- 1 teaspoon of baking powder
- A pinch of salt
- 3 eggs

- 1 teaspoon of vanilla extract

- 1 teaspoon of almond extract

- 1 cup of preserved almonds

Instructions:

1. Preheat your oven to around 350°.

2. Place the almonds on a baking sheet and toast them in the oven for 10 minutes, then let them cool.

3. Prepare the dough by mixing the flour, sugar, baking powder, and salt in a container.

4. Crack the eggs in a separate bowl, add vanilla and almond extract, and beat them well.

5. Pour the beaten eggs on the dough slowly as you keep mixing the entire thing.

6. Add the toasted almonds one by one so they are evenly distributed throughout the dough.

7. Shape the dough into biscotti logs, each about 12 inches long and two inches thick.

8. Place the logs on a baking sheet, leaving an inch of space between each, and place the sheet in the preheated oven.

9. Bake for around half an hour.

10. Let them cool for 15 minutes before slicing each piece diagonally.

11. Place the pieces on the baking sheet, then cut the sides facing down.

12. Bring down the temperature of the oven to 325° and bake the biscuits again for 15 minutes.

13. Let them cool, and serve immediately after.

Rosemary Walnuts

This is probably the easiest walnut recipe out there. You can enhance the taste of regular walnuts within 20 minutes.

Ingredients:

- 2 cups of preserved walnuts
- A pinch or two of salt
- A pinch or two of cayenne pepper
- 2 teaspoons of crushed rosemary

Instructions:

1. Split the walnuts into two halves.
2. Place the pieces in a bowl.
3. Sprinkle salt, pepper, and rosemary.
4. Toss or stir for even distribution.
5. Arrange a single layer on a baking sheet so there is no overlap.
6. Preheat the oven to 350°, and bake the nuts for 10 minutes.
7. Either consume them right away or let them cool before transferring them to an airtight jar for long-term storage.

Hazelnut Ice Cream Cheesecake

Hazelnut ice cream cheesecake is the undisputed nut-king of desserts. No other type of nut tastes as good as hazelnuts on cakes and tarts. This ice cream cheesecake tastes like heaven, and it is one of the simplest desserts to prepare. It will take no more than 15 minutes of your time (provided you've already prepared the chocolate hazelnut spread), and it will be ready after a few hours of freezing.

Chocolate Hazelnut Spread (Nutella) Ingredients:

- 7 ounces of preserved hazelnuts
- 5 ounces of milk
- Half a teaspoon of vanilla extract
- A pinch of salt
- 2-3 tablespoons of cocoa powder
- Sugar (as required)
- 2 tablespoons of coconut oil

Instructions:

1. Preheat your oven to 350°.
2. Place the hazelnuts on a baking sheet and bake in the oven for 10 minutes.
3. Let them cool for another 10 minutes, then rub them in a towel to remove the outer skin.
4. Process them in a food processor for five minutes.
5. Add milk, vanilla extract, cocoa powder, sugar, and salt and process them again for three minutes.

Hazelnut Ice Cream Cheesecake Ingredients:

- 7 ounces of honey-nut cornflakes
- 25-30 ounces of chocolate hazelnut spread
- 12-13 ounces of full-fat cream cheese
- 1 tablespoon of preserved hazelnuts

Instructions:

1. Mix and beat cornflakes and eight ounces of spread in a container.
2. Transfer this to a cake pan, and make the surface even.
3. In another container, beat the cream cheese as you add the remaining spread.
4. Pour it over the cornflake base and smooth it out.
5. Cover it with a thin film and keep it in the freezer for a few hours or until the dessert becomes soft enough to cut with a knife.
6. Press the remaining hazelnuts evenly throughout and enjoy the taste.

You can directly purchase Nutella from the supermarket, but why spend money on something you can easily prepare at home? As an added bonus, you get to dabble with more nuts!

Pistachio Energy Balls

These nutritious, energy-packed balls are the perfect snack to kickstart your early morning workout. You can also exhaust your collection of dates with this recipe. It will take you just over an hour to prepare 12 to 14 energy balls.

Ingredients:

- 1 cup of pistachios
- 5-6 dates
- 1 ounce of coconut (shredded and sweetened)
- 1.5 ounces of rolled oats
- 1-2 teaspoons of vegetable oil
- Honey (as required)
- Salt (as required)

Instructions:

1. Place a single layer of pistachios on a baking sheet.
2. Preheat your oven to 375° and place the sheet inside.
3. Toast for around 10 minutes.
4. Process the nuts in a food processor until no large pieces remain.
5. Transfer 2 tablespoons of the pistachios back onto the baking sheet (to be used for coating later).
6. Pour vegetable oil and sprinkle salt over the remaining pistachios in the processor.
7. Keep processing for 10 more minutes.
8. Pour the mixture into a container.
9. Add dates, shredded coconut, oats, and honey, and beat the concoction until it is properly mixed.
10. Create 1-inch thick balls from the resultant dough.
11. Roll each ball over the pistachios you kept aside in step 5.

12. Place them on a plate without touching each other.

13. Keep the plate in the fridge for around half an hour.

To store these scrumptious energy balls for later, seal them in a jar and keep them in a cool, dry place. For a more enriched taste, add a pinch of salt with a larger pinch of kosher salt. Vegetable oil can be substituted with olive oil or avocado oil.

Chapter 8: Beyond Preservation: Creative Uses for Preserved Foods

Preserved foods can sometimes get a negative reputation for tasting horrible and being bad for your health. This perception couldn't be further from the truth. There are thousands of great dishes you can prepare with preserved food, and when included in a holistic diet, they have tons of nutritional value. For example, sauerkraut, which is fermented cabbage, is a brilliant probiotic. Sauerkraut creates healthy gut bacteria that aid in digestion. Furthermore, it can lower the risks of getting various diseases, and it has even been known to assist with weight loss. Therefore, processed food does not always have to be viewed as unhealthy. If you preserve your own food, you can maximize the health benefits by using natural preservatives.

10. Combining preserved food with fresh food can help you meet your nutritional needs. Source: https://unsplash.com/photos/cooked-rice-with-egg-ykThMylLsbY?utm_content=creditShareLink&utm_medium=referral&utm_source=unsplash

By combining preserved food with fresh food in creative ways, you can construct a diet that meets all your nutritional needs. You can also learn new ways to prepare food to impress even the harshest critics. The tips and recipes outlined in this chapter will give you adaptable meal ideas so you do not get bored eating repetitive food. Learning new ways of cooking can be daunting, but with the right guidance, you can kick down that fear and use simple ingredients to craft restaurant-quality dishes.

You wouldn't want to find yourself in the position of having shelves stocked with preserved food but having nothing to cook with it. The preservation methods are only the first step in exploring this new world of culinary art. People use food as a medium for so many social exchanges. Whether it is a family gathering, a date, a barbeque among friends, grabbing a quick lunch with colleagues, or even an apology chocolate basket, food permeates so many aspects of human life. Therefore, incorporating foods that you have processed and preserved into these social elements of eating can create a sense of accomplishment, filling you with joy. There's nothing quite like looking at someone licking their lips and fingers clean from the sheer satisfaction of eating a meal you cooked. That self-care moment when you carefully plate your food with a glass of your favorite drink before putting on an entertaining show while maybe lighting a scented candle will just be bolstered when you include food that you have preserved.

So, get ready to dive into a multitude of unique recipes using the many kinds of preservation techniques that you have learned. These recipes include food that has been fermented, pickled, brined, and smoked. The options of recipes and tips can be arranged to suit your lifestyle and taste preferences. Whether you want to whip up something fancy or just throw together a quick snack, every option is catered to you with easy-to-follow instructions that provide you with the in-depth details that you need. Once you have the basics down, you can start experimenting to put your twist on incredible meals to take them to the next level. There is no need to run from the stove and oven because you are afraid of the unknown. With these simple meals, your hand will be held to lead you to either becoming the perfect preservation chef or adding to the arsenal of recipes you already have under your belt.

Cooking with Preserved Ingredients

You may already be cooking with preserved ingredients without even realizing it. For example, putting a pickle on a delicious cheeseburger adds that tangy sourness to the salty and meaty creaminess of the rest of the ingredients. The preservation process affects the taste of the item. For example, a pickled vegetable would be sour, and brine could add saltiness to a dish. Therefore, one of the major keys to cooking with preserved food is understanding how to use the taste that the preservation has embedded in the ingredients. Just as a pickle beautifully compliments a burger, your preserved food can be used to enhance the flavor of your favorite dish.

In some cases, the preservation method is central to the flavor. For example, using smoked meat, cheese, or vegetables in your meal can become the centerpiece of the dish. The smokiness is complimented by the food surrounding it, so you can cater your recipe to match the smoky flavor. Therefore, your preserved food does not always have to be a side or garnish, like in the case of a pickle. The big items that form the body of your dish can also be preserved.

In the modern age, people predominantly use preserved food as opposed to fresh ingredients. It is normal to pour food out of a can or a jar to make an amazing dish. The only difference is the personality attached to preserving your food. The vacuum-sealed, plastic-packed, mass-produced preserved options bought from supermarket chains seem cold and lifeless, filled with corporate distance and indifference. Removing what you have preserved from the packaging to use it to feed yourself and your family just has a sprinkle of more personality because it comes from the soul.

How you preserve your food also alters its nutritional value. For example, the fermentation process adds healthy bacteria to a meal that acts as a probiotic. The gut biome is central to your health. If you have great digestion, there is a knock-on effect that increases your overall well-being because now, your body is better able to absorb all the nutrients in the food. Furthermore, some people have suggested that when you adjust your microbiome, your mood and thoughts can change as well, and you will begin having healthier cravings.

The reason why preserved food has taken over the market is convenience. Being able to store food longer gives you the ability to stockpile ingredients, which means fewer trips to the store or the garden if you are preserving the freshest produce. Fresh food decomposes and rots relatively quickly if you do not store it in a refrigerator. Even then, a preserved option in the fridge will outlive the fresh choice. There are many health benefits to fresh food, so it is not advisable to remove it completely from your diet. However, when coupled with some preserved food that you have made yourself in the healthiest way possible, your diet can be taken to new heights of taste and nutrition. These benefits can only come from the support of the various processes you have undertaken to make your food last longer. Cooking with preserved food means exploiting its health and taste benefits in combination with the upsides of fresh food in order to create a holistic super diet that is both beneficial and pleasurable.

Unique Recipes and Dishes

Sometimes, you just want to put something together quickly, but on other occasions, you really want to put your best foot forward and cook something with a bit more pizazz. Impressing people with your culinary skills does not need to break the bank or lead you to burn your kitchen down with complications. Preserved food can easily be introduced into unique recipes that will have you feeling like Gordon Ramsay without the foul language and attitude.

The complex and layered tastes of a variety of preserved foods can be creatively exploited to come up with surprisingly delicious taste variations. The subtleties of the flavors of your preserved additions to a meal come through in a way that can propel a meal over the top. Unique flavor combinations take you on a culinary journey of awakening to taste beyond the salty sweetness of a typical fast food diet. Putting some time and effort into exploring the uncharted territory of unfamiliar ingredients places you at the forefront of diversifying your diet for the better.

People eat with all their senses. Different preservation techniques give you additional methods to alter the taste, smell, texture, and look of a meal. Therefore, like a kitchen ninja, your abilities are expanded because you have a vast selection of culinary weapons to draw from that will knock someone's taste buds straight into heaven. The new complexities of aromas and flavors you create with preservation bring an unmistakable depth to your cooking.

Many traditional meals in different cultures include preserved foods as key ingredients. Therefore, you can broaden your geographic and cultural horizons as well when you submerge yourself in the artistry of cooking with products you have preserved. Once you have some traditional recipes perfected, you can create fusion dishes that bring different parts of the world together in a taste explosion. Bravery and experimentation are the mark of any great cook. Do not be afraid to fail because the first time you try a complicated recipe, you are likely to mess it up. Learn from your mistakes and move forward so that you can grow as a wizard in the kitchen.

Commercial preservation is useful, and it can be substituted in these recipes, but it does not quite have the same effect as something you worked to preserve yourself. It's like the difference between buying your house and building a home with your own hands. Yes, at the end of the day, you are still going to enjoy the comfort of a house whether you have built it yourself or bought it, but walking through the hallways looking at your own handiwork as you caress the walls is a different kind of fulfillment and sense of accomplishment.

As you embrace and try the following recipes, pay attention to the complexities of flavor and how different combinations of sweet, sour, salty, smoky, and bitter work together. These dishes are meant for savoring, so eat slowly as every note and highlight dance on your tongue. These unique meals using preserved ingredients that you can make yourself will set you apart as a home chef not to be reckoned with.

Smoked Pork Belly

A steaming smoked pork belly on a Sunday afternoon, with some mash and gravy on the side, sounds like home. This comfort food will leave your belly full, with that warm, sleepy feeling you get after a Thanksgiving dinner. The low and slow barbeque of a good smoker gives you unparalleled flavor as the charred wood penetrates deep into the fibers of the meat. The crisp outer layer, with the juicy inside, is a wonderful balance of textures that is a beautiful culinary experience. The sweetness of the pork, the spiciness of the seasoning, and the smokiness of the barbeque work together to give you an unforgettable palate. This meal is perfectly suited for a large group of people, so have fun while you eat and connect with the people you love.

Ingredients:

- Dry rub of your choice
- Pork belly
- Your choice of hickory, maple, or oak wood, but it is best to use a combination of the three for a deep and complex smoke

Instructions:

1. Start by using a sharp knife to remove the skin from your pork belly.

2. Cover your meat with your dry rub, and massage it into the pork to make sure every inch of the surface is covered.

3. Wrap it tightly with plastic, ensuring that there are no air bubbles, and place it in the fridge for 12 to 24 hours so that the flavor can sink deep into the meat.

4. Remove your pork belly from the fridge, unwrap it, and allow it to sit on the counter until it reaches room temperature.

5. Insert your wood into your smoker and heat it until it reaches 225°F.

6. Smoke your pork over an indirect fire for about four hours until the internal temperature reaches 165°F.

7. Allow the pork belly to rest for about 30 minutes before slicing into the juicy cut.

8. Serve as is or with your choice of starch and salads.

Turkey Brine

Turkey brine is a delicious alternative to cooking this big, wonderful bird outside of the traditional stuffing roast that is usually done. The delicious, sour, and salty flavor will have you smacking your lips and singing the praises of this recipe, wondering why you hadn't tried it sooner. Your homemade brine made of salt and seasoning can be put to good use with this turkey recipe. Whether it is a weekend with friends or a holiday with family, this turkey recipe is sure to be a hit at the dinner table. With this delicious recipe, you would be lucky to find a crumb of leftovers to take home.

Ingredients:

- 1 cup of apple cider
- 2 gallons of water
- Half a handful of fresh rosemary leaves
- 3 to 4 cloves of fresh, chopped garlic
- 1 ½ cups of kosher salt
- 2 cups of brown sugar
- Peppercorns
- Bay leaves
- Orange peels from three large fruits

Instructions:

1. Mix all your ingredients in a large pot and boil the combination.
2. Slowly stir until all the sugar and salt are completely dissolved.

3. Place your raw turkey in a pot and cover it with the brine mixture. Refrigerate for 24 hours to allow the turkey to absorb the goodness of the mixture.

4. Remove the turkey from the brine and rinse thoroughly, removing any excess salt or ingredients clinging to the flesh.

5. Pat dry and pre-heat your oven to 425°F.

6. Roast your turkey for about an hour, then turn down the heat to 325°F and cook the bird until it is ready.

7. Serve with sides of your choice.

Pickled Eggs and Onions

This recipe is great for a starter or a table snack to nibble on as you kick back and watch your favorite show or sports team. Pickled eggs and onions can also make an incredible side that enhances many dishes. The smack of sourness combined with a bite of a starchy meal is an unexpectedly great combination. This snack is something you can keep neatly packed away in the refrigerator for months before pulling it out whenever you need to or when the craving strikes.

Ingredients:

- A dozen large eggs
- 1 onion
- 1 cup of white vinegar
- 1 cup of water
- 8 to ten cloves of fresh garlic

- ¼ cup of white sugar

Instructions:

1. Hard boil your eggs and chop your onion. Do not slice your onion too finely, and keep big chunks.

2. Cool your eggs in cold water, and then peel off the shells carefully.

3. Mix the rest of your ingredients in a saucepan and boil them for 15 minutes.

4. Allow the pickle mixture to cool before pouring it over your eggs.

5. Cover the eggs with a lid and keep them in the fridge for about a week.

6. Your pickled eggs and onion are now ready to serve.

Strawberry Mojito Kombucha Cocktail

Kombucha is an amazing health drink that contains many antioxidants as well as probiotic qualities. The fermented drink aids in digestion and boosts your immune system. There are some fun ways to drink kombucha that break from the yoga pants-wearing, health guru norm. This refreshing drink has summer written all over it. You can get a bit of a buzz going with this low-sugar drink, but if you do not consume alcohol, omit it from the recipe, and the drink will still be just as delicious.

Ingredients:

- 5 to ten mint leaves
- 2 tablespoons of freshly squeezed lime juice
- 4 ounces of white rum

- 12 ounces of kombucha

- Soda water

- Ice

- Strawberries

Instructions:

1. Crush your strawberries, mint leaves, and lime juice in a bowl until they form a puree. You can use a blender for this step as well.

2. Add your kombucha and white rum.

3. Stir the mixture before pouring it over some ice in an aesthetic glass. You are now ready to get sipping under the summer sun.

4. Omit the white rum for the non-alcoholic mocktail version.

Cape Malay Pickled Fish

This dish is a South African delicacy that is traditionally enjoyed during Easter time. The sour and spicy combination, coupled with the tasty hake, goes together surprisingly well. Impress your friends and family with this exotic dish that will take their pallets away from what they are used to. This recipe goes well with sweet bread to balance out the predominantly sour flavor.

Ingredients:

- Vegetable oil

- 3 pounds of hake fish

- Salt

- 2 to 3 sliced onions
- 2 cloves of finely chopped garlic
- 1 red chili pepper
- 5 bay leaves
- Peppercorns
- Whole allspice berries
- 2 cups of brown vinegar
- ½ cup of water
- 2 tablespoons of ground cumin, turmeric powder, coriander seed powder, and curry powder
- ½ cup of brown sugar

Instructions:

1. Start by frying your fish in a hot skillet.
2. Next, add your onions and garlic to the pan, cooking them until they are transparent.
3. Add your peppercorns, bay leaves, allspice berries, and chili to the mix.
4. Pour in your water, brown sugar, and vinegar, and bring the mixture to a boil while stirring to dissolve the sugar.
5. Season with the rest of your powdered ingredients.
6. Allow the mixture to cool before pouring the ingredients into a sealable dish.
7. Refrigerate for 24 hours, and you are ready to serve. The longer you keep the mixture in the fridge, the more the pickle will be absorbed by the fish,

creating a more intense flavor. The preservation of this dish allows it to be consumed months after it has been prepared.

Incorporating Preserved Foods into Modern Cuisine

Most people are busy with work, school, or other projects. Life moves extremely fast in the modern world, so many people avoid cooking altogether. This can lead to an unhealthy lifestyle of fast food and junk, wreaking all kinds of havoc on your system. Therefore, it is essential to have nutritious dishes you can prepare quickly for when you are tired, in a rush, or on the move. Modern food is all about convenience, so it helps to have some recipes you can throw together in a few minutes.

A lot of people have their entire day taken up by their work hours. That's why it is beneficial to have something you can prepare in the short time you spend at home in the morning or evening. Besides convenience, modern food is about variety. The globalized world has spoiled people with culinary choices. A walk down any main street in a big city will give you options from all around the world, including Thai, Mexican, Chinese, Indian, and Italian food. The following recipes will give you options from across the globe that can go from a collection of ingredients to a five-star meal in only a few minutes.

By having a selection of meals you can prepare quickly using preserved food, you can add the health benefits of your processed food while enjoying the convenience of a simple recipe. Sometimes, you just don't have the patience to keep looking into a cookbook to figure out the complicated ways to cook unfamiliar meals. With these quick and easy recipes, you can memorize the simple process and use the recipes as a crutch of convenience when you are tired or lazy. In this economy, ordering in may not always be an option. Save your money by cooking at home in a smart way that maximizes cheap ingredients to produce enjoyable meals.

These recipes are adaptable, and they can be catered to specialized diets like vegan and vegetarian. By substituting the basic ingredients, you can adapt these meals to match your eating habits. Furthermore, if you are a fit and health-conscious person who regularly attends the gym, you can add some of these dishes as part of your meal prep because of how nutritious they are.

Kimchi Fried Rice

Fried rice is a quick meal that you can make with leftovers. Adding kimchi to this convenient dish exponentially increases its uniqueness and complex flavors. Kimchi is a spicy Korean fermented cabbage that is either a great snack on its own or combined with other meals as a side. Fried rice is the perfect meal for the modern professional whose time is always finely sliced. Furthermore, the meal traditionally uses leftover rice, so it is a way to prevent yourself from wasting food, and it can also help you save money. From start to finish, this meal takes a maximum of 15 minutes, so you can quickly whip it up after a long day of work.

Ingredients:

- Sesame oil

- Kimchi

- Garlic

- Leftover/Day-old rice

- Soy sauce

- Chili Paste

Instructions:

1. Finely chop your onions, kimchi, and garlic.

2. Put your sesame oil into a large, non-stick skillet and bring it to medium heat.

3. Sauté your onions, garlic, and kimchi.

4. Once your vegetables are cooked, lower the heat, add some kimchi juice, and allow your ingredients to simmer for a couple of minutes.

5. Add your cooked rice to the skillet and fry until it is nicely toasted.

6. Add a tablespoon of soy sauce, mix it in, and turn off the heat.

7. To spice up the dish, you can add scrambled eggs, shrimp, or pork, but the meal is beautifully flavored with the kimchi on its own.

Beef Reuben Sandwich

The beef Reuben sandwich is a hearty New York staple. This filling sandwich is deliciously meaty and cheesy, which is all anybody could ask of a sandwich. This ten-minute meal can quickly be prepared either for dinner or lunch. Furthermore, it is easy to pack, so you can enjoy the sandwich while you are on the move. A quick nibble while you are sitting in frustrating traffic is what this meal is made for. The sourness of the sauerkraut subtly breaks through the heartiness of the beef to create a perfectly-balanced sandwich.

Ingredients:

- 6 ounces of pastrami, which is a cured beef brisket
- 2 tablespoons of butter
- 4 slices of rye bread
- 4 slices of Swiss cheese
- ½ cup of drained sauerkraut
- Thousand Island sauce

Instructions:

1. Start by buttering your bread.
2. Place your first slice of bread butter-side down on a non-stick skillet at medium heat.
3. Spread on some Thousand Island sauce.
4. Layer on your pastrami and cheese.
5. Top with your sauerkraut, and then add the other slice on top. Flip to toast the other side, and your sandwich is ready.
6. Repeat the process, and you'll have two incredible beef Reuben sandwiches to either share or enjoy alone, depending on how hungry you are.

Fried Pickles

This guilty pleasure is quick and easy to make while being filled with all the deep-fried deliciousness that you need. The salty, sour crunch is an awesome snack when returning from a night out or even when you just want to kick up your feet on a day off. This tasty snack is a great party treat that can be put together in no time when you have guests over. Either a spicy or a creamy dipping sauce compliments fried pickles so well that you will not be able to stop once you start popping them. Heat that oil and get ready to have one of the tastiest fried treats you'll ever try.

Ingredients:

- Vegetable oil
- 2 cups of flour
- ¼ cup of cornstarch
- Salt
- Pepper
- Paprika
- Onion powder
- Garlic powder
- ¼ cup of cornstarch
- 1 cup of buttermilk
- Dill pickles
- Ranch dressing or your choice of dipping sauce

Instructions:

1. Start by draining the liquid from your dill pickles and patting them dry.

2. Heat your vegetable oil in a skillet until it reaches about 375°F.

3. Mix your flour and cornstarch with 1 teaspoon of pepper, ½ teaspoon of paprika, salt to taste, and ½ teaspoon of onion and garlic powder.

4. Mix your egg with your buttermilk in a separate bowl.

5. Thinly slice your pickles horizontally.

6. Dip your pickles into the buttermilk mixture and then coat them with the dry powder mix. Deep fry them until golden crispy and serve with a dipping sauce. This snack is best enjoyed when consumed immediately.

Conclusion

Food preservation radically shifted society and advanced civilization. The more food humans were able to keep, the better it was in the winter months when there was limited growth taking place in agrarian cultures. Preservation also allowed people to travel further, carrying food supplies and assisting humanity to expand into new territories. Today, preserved food can be bought on the shelves of grocery stores in cans, tins, and dehydrated options packaged for your convenience. Furthermore, technology like refrigeration has greatly expanded preservation capabilities. However, there is nothing quite like taking fresh produce and processing it yourself.

Preservation is all about controlling the microbiome of your food. For example, in the fermentation process, you are using microorganisms to convert starch and carbohydrates into either alcohol or consumable acids so that the food can last longer. Drying food manipulates the water content of your produce to make the environment inhospitable for bacteria and other microbes. Pickling and brining also kill certain microorganisms, so that your food can be stored longer. Cold storage methods limit the growth of various microbes in order to maintain edible food for an extended period. The bottom line of all these preservation methods is understanding the unseen world of your food so that you can intervene and manipulate it to your benefit.

Knowing multiple preservation recipes and techniques allows you to tap into the mini world of microbes in your food in different ways according to your needs and desires. Depending on how long you want to store your food, what you have access to, and your personal preference, you can adopt the methods you have learned through the book according to whatever suits you. Food preservation seems intimidating to some, but once you have a basic understanding of the underlying science and the practical knowledge, you can start practicing to quickly become a food preservation master.

The convenience of preserved food is undeniable, which is why the shelves in supermarkets are piled to the ceiling with various kinds of processed products. However, purchasing these items will never be as fulfilling as preserving your own food. Furthermore, you can monitor and control your ingredients, which allows you to be in a better position to make healthier choices. You have more control to make ethical decisions because you are involved in every step of the process, so you can minimize exploitative practices that are rife in the food industry. Therefore, preserving your food can extend beyond a fun hobby to a mindful practice for you to improve society and your health one small choice at a time.

References

5 traditional food processing techniques explained. (2013, August 8). FutureLearn. https://www.futurelearn.com/info/courses/how-is-my-food-made/0/steps/63303

A guide to brining. (2015, August 25). Morton Salt. https://www.mortonsalt.com/article/a-guide-to-brining/

Ajmera, R., MS, & RD. (2022, April 21). How to dehydrate food: Methods, benefits, tips, and more. Healthline. https://healthline.com/nutrition/dehydrated-food

Almond biscotti. (n.d.). Taste of Home. https://www.tasteofhome.com/recipes/almond-biscotti/

Alyssa. (2023, January 17). How to make nut butter. Simply Quinoa. https://www.simplyquinoa.com/how-to-make-nut-butter/

Anampiu, P. (2023, February 25). *How To Make Dehydrated Fish In A Food Dehydrator*. Dehydrated Cookbook. https://dehydratedcookbook.com/dehydrated-fish/

Baldwin, D. (2023, October 10). The must-have dehydrating tools you really need. The Purposeful Pantry. https://thepurposefulpantry.com/dehydrating-tools-you-really-need/

Bond, W. (2019, June 13). Kimchi Fried Rice. Whitneybond.com. https://whitneybond.com/kimchi-fried-rice/

Boyer, R., Extension specialist, Huff, V. T. K., graduate student, & Tech, V. (n.d.). Using dehydration to preserve fruits, vegetables, and meats. Ext.vt.edu. https://pubs.ext.vt.edu/content/dam/pubs_ext_vt_edu/348/348-597/348-597(FST-304NP).pdf

Bubel, M. A. N. (2022, September 30). DIY Root Cellar: Cold Storage Basics. Mother Earth News – The Original Guide To Living Wisely. https://www.motherearthnews.com/real-food/fundamentals-of-root-cellaring-zm0z91zsie/

Classic Beef Reuben Sandwich. (n.d.). Beefitswhatsfordinner.com. https://www.beefitswhatsfordinner.com/recipes/recipe/55599/classic-beef-reuben-sandwich

Cobbins, R. (n.d.). Ambrosia salad. Taste of Home. https://www.tasteofhome.com/recipes/ambrosia-salad/

Content, Z. (2023, September 18). Mastering pickling: A beginner's guide to the pickling process 2023. Two Brothers Organic Farms. https://twobrothersindiashop.com/blogs/food-health/a-guide-to-pickling-process

Cookist. (2022, April 6). How to store jams, pickled vegetables, and chutneys. Cookist. https://www.cookist.com/how-to-store-jams-pickled-vegetables-and-chutneys/

De Cicco, D. (2010, June 21). Pickled vegetable basics. SheKnows. https://www.sheknows.com/food-and-recipes/articles/815835/pickled-vegetable-basics-1/

Dehydrating food: Is it good for you? (n.d.). WebMD. https://www.webmd.com/diet/dehydrating-food-good-for-you

Desmazery, B. (n.d.). Chocolate hazelnut ice cream cheesecake. BBC Good Food. https://www.bbcgoodfood.com/recipes/chocolate-hazelnut-ice-cream-cheesecake

Douglas, E. (n.d.). How to Salt Fish. Ehow.com. Retrieved January 11, 2024, from https://ehow.com/how_7331153_salt-fish.html

Drummond, R. (2023, November 9). Ree's turkey brine recipe is the key to your best Thanksgiving bird yet. The Pioneer Woman. https://www.thepioneerwoman.com/food-cooking/recipes/a11882/my-favorite-turkey-brine/

Drying food at home. (n.d.). Umn.edu. https://extension.umn.edu/preserving-and-preparing/drying-food

Duffett, B. (2018, July 6). How to dehydrate fruits and vegetables for a healthy snack. EatingWell. https://www.eatingwell.com/article/290910/how-to-dehydrate-fruits-and-vegetables-for-a-healthy-snack/

Ecotutu. (2022, February 23). Food preservation: The effect on our health and economy. Linkedin.com. https://www.linkedin.com/pulse/food-preservation-effect-our-health-economy-ecotutu

EIT Food. (n.d.). 5 traditional food processing techniques explained. FutureLearn. https://www.futurelearn.com/info/courses/how-is-my-food-made/0/steps/63303

Farm, F. H. (n.d.). Food preserving - dehydration. Fruithillfarm.com. https://www.fruithillfarm.com/info/2023/07/food-preserving-dehydration/

Fellows, P. J. (2017). Smoking. In Food Processing Technology (pp. 717–732). Elsevier.

Fmt Magazine. (2023, January 11). Why do we need to preserve food? The importance of food. Medium. https://fmtmagazines.medium.com/why-do-we-need-to-preserve-food-the-importance-of-food-5b985540b535

Food Insight. (2017, October 3). The benefits of preservatives in our food –. Food Insight. https://foodinsight.org/the-benefits-of-preservatives-in-our-food/

Fresh Off The Grid. (2020, May 21). The ultimate guide to dehydrating food. Fresh Off The Grid. https://www.freshoffthegrid.com/dehydrating-food/

Frozen fruit smoothies. (2015, September 4). Foodnetwork.com. https://www.foodnetwork.com/recipes/food-network-kitchen/frozen-fruit-smoothies-recipe-1914927

Garlic pickled eggs. (n.d.). Allrecipes. https://www.allrecipes.com/recipe/23928/garlic-pickled-eggs/

Goode, G. (2023, August 17). Fried pickles. The Pioneer Woman. https://www.thepioneerwoman.com/food-cooking/recipes/a35880840/fried-pickles-recipe/

Hassing, S. (2019, May 21). Low-Sugar Strawberry Mojito Kombucha Cocktail. The Real Food Dietitians. https://therealfooddietitians.com/strawberry-mojito-kombucha-cocktail/

Helm, J. (2023, March 20). Myth vs. Fact: Fermented Foods. U.S.News. https://health.usnews.com/health-news/blogs/eat-run/articles/myth-vs-fact-fermented-foods

Henry, J.-L. (2021, November 4). How to ferment fruits (plus a fermented plums recipe!). Revolution Fermentation. https://revolutionfermentation.com/en/blogs/fermented-vegetables/how-ferment-fruits/

Herringshaw, D. (2015). Drying Fruits and Vegetables. Osu.edu. https://ohioline.osu.edu/factsheet/HYG-5347

Home Storage of Fruits and Vegetables in Root Cellars. (n.d.). Missouri.Edu. https://extension.missouri.edu/publications/mp562

How to Preserve Food Safely in a Root Cellar? (2022, October 28). Ruuvi. https://ruuvi.com/root-cellar/

Introduction to food dehydration. (n.d.). Missouri.edu. https://extension.missouri.edu/publications/gh1562

Josh. (2020, November 14). Types of pickling methods and how you can do them at home. Pickle Wiki. https://picklewiki.com/?p=167

Josh. (2022, July 22). How to pickle fruits so that they taste amazing. Pickle Wiki. https://picklewiki.com/?p=245

Klein, J. (2021, December 7). How smoked meat can be kept for a long time. American Made Grills.

https://americanmadegrills.com/blogs/grilling-tips/how-smoked-meat-can-be-kept-for-a-long-time

Krezevska, T. (2017, January 31). Dehydrating123: How to dehydrate meat for backpacking meals. Trail Recipes. https://trail.recipes/dehydrating123/dehydrating123-how-to-dehydrate-meat-for-backpacking-meals/

Landis, L. (2011, September 16). Summer peach and balsamic pizza. Love and Olive Oil. https://www.loveandoliveoil.com/2011/09/summer-peach-and-balsamic-pizza.html

Leaf, L. (2022, September 28). How to smoke fish. Themeateater.com; MeatEater. https://www.themeateater.com/cook/cooking-techniques/how-to-smoke-fish

Life, M. G. (2022, July 20). How to dehydrate fruits and vegetables. MyGardenLife. https://mygardenlife.com/recipes-edibles/how-to-dehydrate-fruits-and-vegetables

Marrone, T. (2020, October 8). Dehydrate red meat and poultry. Mother Earth News – The Original Guide To Living Wisely; Mother Earth News. https://www.motherearthnews.com/real-food/dehydrate-red-meat-poultry-zeoz1811zmcg/

Marrow Private Chefs. (2011, May 15). How to ferment fruit. wikiHow. https://www.wikihow.com/Ferment-Fruit

Masterclass. (2021, July 30). A guide to home food preservation: How to pickle, can, ferment, dry, and preserve at home. Masterclass. https://www.masterclass.com/articles/a-guide-to-home-food-preservation-how-to-pickle-can-ferment-dry-and-preserve-at-home

Melissah, -. (2014, June 5). One-cup slice. Www.bestrecipes.com.au. https://www.bestrecipes.com.au/recipes/one-cup-slice-recipe/v4q7ui7m?r=baking/zvxkjrdx&h=baking

Ned, & Hannah. (2022, March 22). What is food fermentation? The Making Life. https://themakinglife.com/what-is-food-fermentation/

NITSCKIE. (2023, July 18). Cape Malay Pickled Fish. Allrecipes. https://www.allrecipes.com/recipe/104444/cape-malay-pickled-fish/

Nummer, B. A., & Andress, E. L. (2002). *Curing and Smoking Meats for Home Food* Preservation. Nchfp.uga.edu. https://nchfp.uga.edu/publications/nchfp/lit_rev/cure_smoke_post proc.html

Nunez, K. (n.d.). Basic Jam. Martha Stewart. https://www.marthastewart.com/1128024/basic-jam-recipe

Nutritionist, J. W. –. (2023, May 16). Top 7 health benefits of fermenting. BBC Good Food. https://www.bbcgoodfood.com/howto/guide/health-benefits-offermenting

Ohioline. (2015a, May 28). Food Preservation: Basics for Canning Fruit. Ohioline.osu.edu. https://ohioline.osu.edu/factsheet/HYG-5343

Ohioline. (2015b, May 28). Food Preservation: Freezing Fruits. Ohioline.osu.edu. https://ohioline.osu.edu/factsheet/HYG-5349

Pistachio Energy Balls. (n.d.). Food Network. Retrieved January 11, 2024, from https://www.foodnetwork.com/recipes/food-network-kitchen/pistachio-energy-balls-11114076

Page, T. (2020, January 18). Root Cellaring 101 - What is a Root Cellar, Ideal Conditions, and Use. Homestead Honey. https://homestead-honey.com/root-cellaring-101-what-is-a-root-cellar-ideal-conditions-and-use/

Porter, B. (2019, May 29). 9 benefits of dehydrating food that may surprise you. The Seasonal Homestead. https://www.theseasonalhomestead.com/9-benefits-of-dehydrating-food-that-may-surprise-you/

Pottle, R. (2016, January 2). How to dry vegetables in the oven. Seedtopantry.com; Seed to Pantry. https://seedtopantry.com/2016/01/02/how-to-dry-vegetables-in-the-oven/

Riches, D. (2003, November 12). What to do to brine poultry, fish, and meat. The Spruce Eats. https://www.thespruceeats.com/all-about-brining-331490

Robbins, O. (2021, November 3). Guide to dehydrating food: Methods, foods to try, and recipes. Food Revolution Network. https://foodrevolution.org/blog/how-to-dehydrate-food-guide/

Rooftopgardener. (2023, January 25). An introduction to smoking food preservation method: The pros and cons. Your Food Preservation WIKI; Rooftopgardener. https://makefoodstay.com/smoking-food-preservation-method/

Root Cellars: Types and Storage Tips. (n.d.). Almanac.Com. https://www.almanac.com/content/root-cellars-types-and-storage-tips

Rosemary walnuts. (n.d.). Taste of Home. https://www.tasteofhome.com/recipes/rosemary-walnuts/

Shrader, M. B. (2022, September 17). How to dehydrate vegetables the easy way. Mary's Nest; Mary's Nest, LLC. https://marysnest.com/how-to-dehydrate-vegetables-the-easy-way/

Smoked pork belly. (2018, November 29). Salt Pepper Skillet; Salt Pepper Skillet LLC. https://saltpepperskillet.com/recipes/smoked-pork-belly/

Smoker, B. (2023, January 13). How to smoke vegetables: The guide to everything. Bradley Smoker USA. https://www.bradleysmoker.com/blogs/articles-smoking-guide/how-to-smoke-vegetables-the-guide-to-everything

Stewart, E. (2022, October 3). How to freeze fruit to enjoy all year long. Stasher. https://www.stasherbag.com/blogs/stasher-life/how-to-freeze-fruit

Stewart, G. (2021, March 3). Dehydrating equipment - what you need to get started. Gettystewart.com; Getty Stewart - Professional Home Economist. https://www.gettystewart.com/dehydrating-equipment-what-you-need-to-get-started/

The Cooking Bride. (2018, November 12). The basics of brining. The Cooking Bride. https://cookingbride.com/kitchen-basics/the-basics-of-brining/

The essential equipment for food dehydration: A guide for beginners. (2023, December 2). Dehydrated Foodz. https://dehydratedfoodz.com/equipment-for-food-dehydration/

What are the benefits of fermented foods? (2018, August 20). Heart Foundation NZ. https://www.heartfoundation.org.nz/about-us/news/blogs/fermented-foods-the-latest-trend

What is the Best Wood for Smoking Meat? (n.d.). Chadsbbq.com. https://www.chadsbbq.com/what-is-the-best-wood-for-smoking-meat/

Yule, S. (2022, November 6). How to prepare and preserve nuts to keep them fresh. Morning Chores. https://morningchores.com/how-to-preserve-nuts/

0d9c79f9-7574-4c1b-a750-d2549a60b593R01